# LANGUAGE TARGETS
## TO TEACH A CHILD TO COMMUNICATE

A Resource to Manage
Language Instruction

Diana Luckevich

TalkingWords, Inc.
P.O. Box 743
Mercer Island, WA   98040
(425) 269 – 5775
www.talkingwords.com
info@talkingwords.com

Language Targets to Teach a Child to Communicate is a collection of language examples to teach a child early communication skills.  It is also a student record book to track a student's progress. It is not a language curriculum. There are no recommendations on how to teach a child or when things should be taught. There is no prescribed sequence of instruction. The author highly recommends that the reader use a language curriculum as well as an experienced professional to help make instructional programming decisions for each child.

Printed in the United States of America

10   9  8   7  6  5  4  3  2  1

# Chapter Contents

# Contents

# CHAPTER 2 - VERB .......................................................................... 60

# CHAPTER 3 - RECEPTIVE INSTRUCTION .............................. 71

# CHAPTER 4 - WORD ASSOCIATION ........................................ 75

Language Targets to Teach a Child to Communicate

# Introduction

Language Targets to Teach a Child to Communicate is a tool for managing an intensive early language instruction program.  It is a resource for teachers, therapists, and parents to help students with autism, PDD, Down syndrome or other language delays. This book provides target lists with specific words, phrases and questions to teach children who have no language skills all the way up to those who are learning to have a conversation. These targets help to teach a child basic language skills for meaningful functional communication. There are more than 5,000 targets organized into 190 categories.

This book has two goals. The first goal is to be a reference that provides quick access to language targets for teaching communication. These targets have been carefully selected to support the communication development of early language learners.  The second goal is to enable the collection of data for one student. The data organized in this book makes it easy to track what language a student has learned and when it was mastered. The book can be passed between teachers to provide access to detailed information about a student's language skills. This data collection tool can reduce time spent testing students each year to get baseline language competency data. This book facilitates the planning and management of a student's language objectives.

A language curriculum or an experienced professional should guide decisions about which and when categories in this book should be taught to an individual child. Targets from those selected categories should be chosen based on what is functional for each child.  The targets in each category in this book are listed alphabetically.  However, one does not need to teach the targets in alphabetical order. The order and combination of targets taught to a child should be customized to the child based on their optimal learning style, their functional needs and their language goals.

This book intentionally does not offer instructions or teaching techniques. It simply provides lists of possible language targets to teach.  Please see the reference section of this book for a few recommended instructional books to help you make instructional decisions.

## Data Collection

Language Targets to Teach a Child to Communicate supports the data collection of language progress for an individual student. Each category of targets has a blank line labeled "Objective" to record the instructional purpose of that category for a student.

This book supports target level data collection with three milestones for each target. Milestones refer to how a target is used as a communication tool. The following example shows how some milestones may be recorded for a target in the noun category. Milestones are specified as column headings for a category of targets like this example:

| Target | Receptive Date | Expressive Date | Spontaneous Date |
|--------|----------------|-----------------|------------------|
| ball   | 6/17/04        | 7/12/04         | 8/21/04          |

This example shows three milestones for the target "ball". The Receptive Date indicates when the child receptively learned the word "ball". The Expressive Date records when the child could expressively say "ball". The Spontaneous Date indicates when the child spontaneously labeled or requested a ball. One might consider simply recording a check mark for a milestone instead of a date to record that the child has achieved that milestone for that target or that the child previously knew it.

There are many different milestones that can be recorded. The decision about what milestones to record for each category of target is made by the teacher for the individual student based on the student's abilities and goals. Here are some other possibilities.

### Milestone Examples

| Expressive Start Date | Expressive Mastered Date | Reviewed Date |
|---|---|---|

| Imitates | Says with an Adult | Says with a Peer |
|---|---|---|

| Signs | Picture Exchange | Vocalizes |
|---|---|---|

| Imitates | Mands | Tacts |
|---|---|---|

| One picture | Multiple pictures | Generalized object |
|---|---|---|

| Black line drawing | Color drawing | Real thing |
|---|---|---|

| Matches word to picture | Points to word | Reads word |
|---|---|---|

| Match - Receptive | Imitate – Expressive | Spontaneous Label - Request |
|---|---|---|

The above example shows recording of 6 milestones in 3 columns

# Chapter 1 - Noun

## Accessory

**Objective** _____

| | Target | | | |
|---|---|---|---|---|
| 1 | barrette | | | |
| 2 | belt | | | |
| 3 | bib | | | |
| 4 | bow | | | |
| 5 | bracelet | | | |
| 6 | buckle | | | |
| 7 | button | | | |
| 8 | cap | | | |
| 9 | cowboy hat | | | |
| 10 | earring | | | |
| 11 | fanny pack | | | |
| 12 | glasses | | | |
| 13 | gloves | | | |
| 14 | goggles | | | |
| 15 | hat | | | |
| 16 | head band | | | |
| 17 | helmet | | | |
| 18 | jewelry | | | |
| 19 | key chain | | | |
| 20 | mitten | | | |
| 21 | necklace | | | |
| 22 | pocket | | | |
| 23 | purse | | | |
| 24 | ribbon | | | |
| 25 | ring | | | |
| 26 | scarf | | | |
| 27 | sleeve | | | |
| 28 | snap | | | |
| 29 | sunglasses | | | |
| 30 | tie | | | |
| 31 | umbrella | | | |
| 32 | visor | | | |
| 33 | wallet | | | |
| 34 | watch | | | |
| 35 | zipper | | | |
| 36 | | | | |
| 37 | | | | |
| 38 | | | | |
| 39 | | | | |
| 40 | | | | |

# Aircraft

**Objective** _____

| | **Target** | | | |
|---|---|---|---|---|
| 1 | airplane | | | |
| 2 | blimp | | | |
| 3 | cockpit | | | |
| 4 | glider | | | |
| 5 | helicopter | | | |
| 6 | hot air balloon | | | |
| 7 | jet | | | |
| 8 | parachute | | | |
| 9 | rocket ship | | | |
| 10 | | | | |
| 11 | | | | |
| 12 | | | | |
| 13 | | | | |
| 14 | | | | |
| 15 | | | | |

# Animal

**Objective** _____

| | Target | | | |
|---|---|---|---|---|
| 1 | anteater | | | |
| 2 | ape | | | |
| 3 | armadillo | | | |
| 4 | bat | | | |
| 5 | bear | | | |
| 6 | beaver | | | |
| 7 | buffalo | | | |
| 8 | bull | | | |
| 9 | bunny | | | |
| 10 | calf | | | |
| 11 | camel | | | |
| 12 | cat | | | |
| 13 | cheetah | | | |
| 14 | chimpanzee | | | |
| 15 | chipmunk | | | |
| 16 | colt | | | |
| 17 | cougar | | | |
| 18 | cow | | | |
| 19 | coyote | | | |
| 20 | crocodile | | | |
| 21 | deer | | | |
| 22 | dinosaur | | | |
| 23 | dog | | | |
| 24 | donkey | | | |
| 25 | duck | | | |
| 26 | elephant | | | |
| 27 | elk | | | |
| 28 | ferret | | | |
| 29 | fox | | | |
| 30 | frog | | | |
| 31 | giraffe | | | |
| 32 | goat | | | |
| 33 | gopher | | | |
| 34 | gorilla | | | |
| 35 | guinea pig | | | |
| 36 | hamster | | | |
| 37 | hare | | | |
| 38 | hippopotamus | | | |
| 39 | horse | | | |
| 40 | hyena | | | |

# Animal

**Objective** _____

| Target | | | |
|---|---|---|---|
| 41 iguana | | | |
| 42 jaguar | | | |
| 43 kangaroo | | | |
| 44 kitten | | | |
| 45 koala | | | |
| 46 lamb | | | |
| 47 leopard | | | |
| 48 lion | | | |
| 49 lizard | | | |
| 50 llama | | | |
| 51 lynx | | | |
| 52 mare | | | |
| 53 mole | | | |
| 54 monkey | | | |
| 55 moose | | | |
| 56 mouse | | | |
| 57 mule | | | |
| 58 newt | | | |
| 59 opossum | | | |
| 60 orangutang | | | |
| 61 ox | | | |
| 62 panda | | | |
| 63 panther | | | |
| 64 pig | | | |
| 65 polar bear | | | |
| 66 pony | | | |
| 67 porcupine | | | |
| 68 puppy | | | |
| 69 rabbit | | | |
| 70 raccoon | | | |
| 71 ram | | | |
| 72 rat | | | |
| 73 reindeer | | | |
| 74 reptile | | | |
| 75 rhinoceros | | | |
| 76 sheep | | | |
| 77 skunk | | | |
| 78 snail | | | |
| 79 snake | | | |
| 80 squirrel | | | |

# Animal

**Objective** _____

| Target | | | |
|---|---|---|---|
| 81 stallion | | | |
| 82 tiger | | | |
| 83 toad | | | |
| 84 walrus | | | |
| 85 warthog | | | |
| 86 weasel | | | |
| 87 wolf | | | |
| 88 woodchuck | | | |
| 89 yak | | | |
| 90 zebra | | | |

# Animal ~ Animal Part

**Objective** _____

| Target | | | |
|---|---|---|---|
| 1 antenna | | | |
| 2 beak | | | |
| 3 cage | | | |
| 4 fang | | | |
| 5 feather | | | |
| 6 fin | | | |
| 7 fur | | | |
| 8 gill | | | |
| 9 hoof | | | |
| 10 mane | | | |
| 11 paw | | | |
| 12 scale | | | |
| 13 tail | | | |
| 14 wing | | | |
| 15 whiskers | | | |
| 16 | | | |
| 17 | | | |
| 18 | | | |
| 19 | | | |
| 20 | | | |

# Animal ~ Bird

**Objective** _____

| | Target | | | |
|---|---|---|---|---|
| 1 | bird | | | |
| 2 | chicken | | | |
| 3 | crow | | | |
| 4 | eagle | | | |
| 5 | goose | | | |
| 6 | hen | | | |
| 7 | hummingbird | | | |
| 8 | ostrich | | | |
| 9 | owl | | | |
| 10 | parakeet | | | |
| 11 | parrot | | | |
| 12 | peacock | | | |
| 13 | penguin | | | |
| 14 | pigeon | | | |
| 15 | robin | | | |
| 16 | rooster | | | |
| 17 | seagull | | | |
| 18 | swan | | | |
| 19 | toucan | | | |
| 20 | turkey | | | |
| 21 | | | | |
| 22 | | | | |
| 23 | | | | |
| 24 | | | | |
| 25 | | | | |
| 26 | | | | |
| 27 | | | | |
| 28 | | | | |
| 29 | | | | |
| 30 | | | | |

# Animal ~ Insect

**Objective** _____

| | Target | | | |
|---|---|---|---|---|
| 1 | ant | | | |
| 2 | bee | | | |
| 3 | beetle | | | |
| 4 | bug | | | |
| 5 | butterfly | | | |
| 6 | catepillar | | | |
| 7 | cockroach | | | |
| 8 | dragonfly | | | |
| 9 | earwig | | | |
| 10 | fly | | | |
| 11 | grasshopper | | | |
| 12 | ladybug | | | |
| 13 | mosquito | | | |
| 14 | moth | | | |
| 15 | praying mantis | | | |
| 16 | spider | | | |
| 17 | wasp | | | |

# Animal ~ Water Animal

**Objective** _____

| | Target | | | |
|---|---|---|---|---|
| 1 | alligator | | | |
| 2 | crab | | | |
| 3 | dolphin | | | |
| 4 | fish | | | |
| 5 | jellyfish | | | |
| 6 | lobster | | | |
| 7 | octopus | | | |
| 8 | otter | | | |
| 9 | sea horse | | | |
| 10 | seal | | | |
| 11 | shark | | | |
| 12 | star fish | | | |
| 13 | turtle | | | |
| 14 | whale | | | |
| 15 | | | | |
| 16 | | | | |
| 17 | | | | |

# Author

**Objective** _____

| | Target | | | |
|---|---|---|---|---|
| 1 | Bill Martin | | | |
| 2 | Cythnia Rylant | | | |
| 3 | David McPhail | | | |
| 4 | Don Freeman | | | |
| 5 | Dr. Seuss | | | |
| 6 | Eric Carle | | | |
| 7 | Eric Hill | | | |
| 8 | Frank Asch | | | |
| 9 | H.A.Rey | | | |
| 10 | Jan Brett | | | |
| 11 | John Burningham | | | |
| 12 | Jonathan London | | | |
| 13 | Laura Numeroff | | | |
| 14 | Marc Brown | | | |
| 15 | Margret Wise Brown | | | |
| 16 | Martha Alexander | | | |
| 17 | Mercer Mayer | | | |
| 18 | Norman Bridwell | | | |
| 19 | Richard Scarry | | | |
| 20 | Syd Hoff | | | |
| 21 | | | | |
| 22 | | | | |
| 23 | | | | |
| 24 | | | | |
| 25 | | | | |
| 26 | | | | |
| 27 | | | | |
| 28 | | | | |
| 29 | | | | |
| 30 | | | | |
| 31 | | | | |
| 32 | | | | |
| 33 | | | | |
| 34 | | | | |
| 35 | | | | |
| 36 | | | | |
| 37 | | | | |
| 38 | | | | |
| 39 | | | | |
| 40 | | | | |

# Bathroom

**Objective** _____

| | Target | | | |
|---|---|---|---|---|
| 1 | bathtub | | | |
| 2 | brush | | | |
| 3 | bubble bath | | | |
| 4 | clippers | | | |
| 5 | comb | | | |
| 6 | dental floss | | | |
| 7 | deodorant | | | |
| 8 | hairdryer | | | |
| 9 | hamper | | | |
| 10 | lipstick | | | |
| 11 | lotion | | | |
| 12 | makeup | | | |
| 13 | mirror | | | |
| 14 | potty | | | |
| 15 | powder | | | |
| 16 | qtips | | | |
| 17 | scale | | | |
| 18 | shampoo | | | |
| 19 | shaver | | | |
| 20 | shaving cream | | | |
| 21 | shower | | | |
| 22 | sink | | | |
| 23 | soap | | | |
| 24 | tissue | | | |
| 25 | toilet | | | |
| 26 | toilet paper | | | |
| 27 | tooth paste | | | |
| 28 | toothbrush | | | |
| 29 | towel | | | |
| 30 | towel bar | | | |
| 31 | tweezers | | | |
| 32 | urinal | | | |
| 33 | wash cloth | | | |
| 34 | wig | | | |
| 35 | | | | |
| 36 | | | | |
| 37 | | | | |
| 38 | | | | |
| 39 | | | | |
| 40 | | | | |

# Bedroom

**Objective** _____

| | Target | | | |
|---|---|---|---|---|
| 1 | bed | | | |
| 2 | blanket | | | |
| 3 | closet | | | |
| 4 | cover | | | |
| 5 | crib | | | |
| 6 | curtains | | | |
| 7 | dresser | | | |
| 8 | hanger | | | |
| 9 | mattress | | | |
| 10 | night light | | | |
| 11 | night stand | | | |
| 12 | pillow | | | |
| 13 | pillowcase | | | |
| 14 | quilt | | | |
| 15 | sheet | | | |
| 16 | | | | |
| 17 | | | | |
| 18 | | | | |
| 19 | | | | |
| 20 | | | | |
| 21 | | | | |
| 22 | | | | |
| 23 | | | | |
| 24 | | | | |
| 25 | | | | |
| 26 | | | | |
| 27 | | | | |
| 28 | | | | |
| 29 | | | | |
| 30 | | | | |
| 31 | | | | |
| 32 | | | | |
| 33 | | | | |
| 34 | | | | |
| 35 | | | | |
| 36 | | | | |
| 37 | | | | |
| 38 | | | | |
| 39 | | | | |
| 40 | | | | |

# Birthday Party

**Objective** _____

| | Target | | | |
|---|---|---|---|---|
| 1 | balloon | | | |
| 2 | banner | | | |
| 3 | birthday cake | | | |
| 4 | birthday hat | | | |
| 5 | bow | | | |
| 6 | candles | | | |
| 7 | card | | | |
| 8 | confetti | | | |
| 9 | decorations | | | |
| 10 | envelope | | | |
| 11 | favors | | | |
| 12 | flame | | | |
| 13 | forks | | | |
| 14 | friends | | | |
| 15 | games | | | |
| 16 | ice cream | | | |
| 17 | invitation | | | |
| 18 | make a wish | | | |
| 19 | napkins | | | |
| 20 | noise maker | | | |
| 21 | pin the tail on the donkey | | | |
| 22 | pinata | | | |
| 23 | plates | | | |
| 24 | presents | | | |
| 25 | ribbon | | | |
| 26 | table cloth | | | |
| 27 | thank you card | | | |
| 28 | wrapping paper | | | |
| 29 | | | | |
| 30 | | | | |
| 31 | | | | |
| 32 | | | | |
| 33 | | | | |
| 34 | | | | |
| 35 | | | | |
| 36 | | | | |
| 37 | | | | |
| 38 | | | | |
| 39 | | | | |
| 40 | | | | |

# Boat

**Objective** _____

| Target | | | |
|---|---|---|---|
| 1  boat | | | |
| 2  bumper boat | | | |
| 3  canoe | | | |
| 4  cruise liner | | | |
| 5  ferry | | | |
| 6  fishing boat | | | |
| 7  jetski | | | |
| 8  lifeboat | | | |
| 9  navy boat | | | |
| 10 raft | | | |
| 11 sailboat | | | |
| 12 ship | | | |
| 13 speed boat | | | |
| 14 submarine | | | |
| 15 tugboat | | | |
| 16 | | | |
| 17 | | | |
| 18 | | | |
| 19 | | | |
| 20 | | | |

# Body of Water

**Objective** _____

| Target | | | |
|---|---|---|---|
| 1  bay | | | |
| 2  brook | | | |
| 3  creek | | | |
| 4  lake | | | |
| 5  ocean | | | |
| 6  pond | | | |
| 7  river | | | |
| 8  stream | | | |
| 9  swamp | | | |
| 10 waterfall | | | |
| 11 | | | |
| 12 | | | |
| 13 | | | |
| 14 | | | |
| 15 | | | |

# Body Part

**Objective** _____

| Target | | | |
|---|---|---|---|
| 1 ankle | | | |
| 2 arm | | | |
| 3 armpit | | | |
| 4 back | | | |
| 5 beard | | | |
| 6 belly | | | |
| 7 belly button | | | |
| 8 body | | | |
| 9 brain | | | |
| 10 butt | | | |
| 11 calf | | | |
| 12 cheek | | | |
| 13 chest | | | |
| 14 chin | | | |
| 15 ear | | | |
| 16 elbow | | | |
| 17 eyebrow | | | |
| 18 eyelash | | | |
| 19 eyelid | | | |
| 20 eyes | | | |
| 21 face | | | |
| 22 feet | | | |
| 23 fingernail | | | |
| 24 fingers | | | |
| 25 fist | | | |
| 26 foot | | | |
| 27 forehead | | | |
| 28 gums | | | |
| 29 hair | | | |
| 30 hands | | | |
| 31 head | | | |
| 32 heart | | | |
| 33 heel | | | |
| 34 knee | | | |
| 35 knuckle | | | |
| 36 leg | | | |
| 37 lips | | | |
| 38 lungs | | | |
| 39 missing tooth | | | |
| 40 mouth | | | |

# Body Part

**Objective** _____

| | Target | | | |
|---|---|---|---|---|
| 41 | muscle | | | |
| 42 | mustache | | | |
| 43 | neck | | | |
| 44 | nose | | | |
| 45 | palm | | | |
| 46 | pinky | | | |
| 47 | pointer | | | |
| 48 | shin | | | |
| 49 | shoulder | | | |
| 50 | skeleton | | | |
| 51 | smile | | | |
| 52 | stomach | | | |
| 53 | sweat | | | |
| 54 | teeth | | | |
| 55 | thigh | | | |
| 56 | throat | | | |
| 57 | thumb | | | |
| 58 | toes | | | |
| 59 | tongue | | | |
| 60 | tummy | | | |
| 61 | waist | | | |
| 62 | wrist | | | |
| 63 | | | | |
| 64 | | | | |
| 65 | | | | |
| 66 | | | | |
| 67 | | | | |
| 68 | | | | |
| 69 | | | | |
| 70 | | | | |
| 71 | | | | |
| 72 | | | | |
| 73 | | | | |
| 74 | | | | |
| 75 | | | | |
| 76 | | | | |
| 77 | | | | |
| 78 | | | | |
| 79 | | | | |
| 80 | | | | |

# Book

**Objective** _____

| | Target | | | |
|---|---|---|---|---|
| 1 | Arthur's Birthday | | | |
| 2 | Arthur's Pet Business | | | |
| 3 | Brown Bear Brown Bear What do you see? | | | |
| 4 | Chicka Chicka Boom Boom | | | |
| 5 | Dr. Seuss's ABC's | | | |
| 6 | Go Dog Go | | | |
| 7 | Goodnight Moon | | | |
| 8 | Green Eggs and Ham | | | |
| 9 | Hop on Pop | | | |
| 10 | I Can Read with my Eyes Shut | | | |
| 11 | Just Me and My Dad | | | |
| 12 | Mr. Brown can Moo.  Can you? | | | |
| 13 | One Fish Two Fish Red Fish Blue Fish | | | |
| 14 | Spot Goes to the Beach | | | |
| 15 | Spot's First Walk | | | |
| 16 | The Cat in the Hat | | | |
| 17 | The Three Bears | | | |
| 18 | The Very Busy Spider | | | |
| 19 | The Very Hungry Catepillar | | | |
| 20 | Where's Spot? | | | |
| 21 | | | | |
| 22 | | | | |
| 23 | | | | |
| 24 | | | | |
| 25 | | | | |
| 26 | | | | |
| 27 | | | | |
| 28 | | | | |
| 29 | | | | |
| 30 | | | | |
| 31 | | | | |
| 32 | | | | |
| 33 | | | | |
| 34 | | | | |
| 35 | | | | |
| 36 | | | | |
| 37 | | | | |
| 38 | | | | |
| 39 | | | | |
| 40 | | | | |

# Clothing

**Objective** _____

| Target | | | |
|---|---|---|---|
| 1  bathing suit | | | |
| 2  coat | | | |
| 3  diaper | | | |
| 4  dress | | | |
| 5  hood | | | |
| 6  jeans | | | |
| 7  laundry | | | |
| 8  long sleeve shirt | | | |
| 9  overalls | | | |
| 10  pajamas | | | |
| 11  pants | | | |
| 12  shirt | | | |
| 13  shorts | | | |
| 14  skirt | | | |
| 15  snowsuit | | | |
| 16  sweat pants | | | |
| 17  sweater | | | |
| 18  sweatshirt | | | |
| 19  tshirt | | | |
| 20  underwear | | | |
| 21  vest | | | |
| 22 | | | |
| 23 | | | |
| 24 | | | |
| 25 | | | |
| 26 | | | |
| 27 | | | |
| 28 | | | |
| 29 | | | |
| 30 | | | |
| 31 | | | |
| 32 | | | |
| 33 | | | |
| 34 | | | |
| 35 | | | |
| 36 | | | |
| 37 | | | |
| 38 | | | |
| 39 | | | |
| 40 | | | |

# Color

**Objective** _____

| Target | | | |
|---|---|---|---|
| 1 beige | | | |
| 2 black | | | |
| 3 blue | | | |
| 4 brown | | | |
| 5 cream | | | |
| 6 cyan | | | |
| 7 fuchsia | | | |
| 8 gold | | | |
| 9 green | | | |
| 10 grey | | | |
| 11 indigo | | | |
| 12 ivory | | | |
| 13 khaki | | | |
| 14 magenta | | | |
| 15 maroon | | | |
| 16 olive | | | |
| 17 orange | | | |
| 18 pink | | | |
| 19 purple | | | |
| 20 red | | | |
| 21 silver | | | |
| 22 tan | | | |
| 23 teal | | | |
| 24 turquoise | | | |
| 25 violet | | | |
| 26 white | | | |
| 27 yellow | | | |
| 28 | | | |
| 29 | | | |
| 30 | | | |
| 31 | | | |
| 32 | | | |
| 33 | | | |
| 34 | | | |
| 35 | | | |
| 36 | | | |
| 37 | | | |
| 38 | | | |
| 39 | | | |
| 40 | | | |

# Community Helper

**Objective** _____

| Target | | | |
|---|---|---|---|
| 1  baker | | | |
| 2  bank teller | | | |
| 3  bus driver | | | |
| 4  butcher | | | |
| 5  carpenter | | | |
| 6  cashier | | | |
| 7  chef | | | |
| 8  clerk | | | |
| 9  coach | | | |
| 10  construction worker | | | |
| 11  dentist | | | |
| 12  doctor | | | |
| 13  eye doctor | | | |
| 14  farmer | | | |
| 15  fire fighter | | | |
| 16  garbage man | | | |
| 17  hair stylist | | | |
| 18  janitor | | | |
| 19  librarian | | | |
| 20  life guard | | | |
| 21  mailman | | | |
| 22  mechanic | | | |
| 23  nun | | | |
| 24  nurse | | | |
| 25  park ranger | | | |
| 26  pilot | | | |
| 27  plumber | | | |
| 28  policeman | | | |
| 29  priest | | | |
| 30  principal | | | |
| 31  receptionist | | | |
| 32  security guard | | | |
| 33  soldier | | | |
| 34  teacher | | | |
| 35  TV reporter | | | |
| 36  vet | | | |
| 37  waiter | | | |
| 38  waitress | | | |
| 39  zoo keeper | | | |
| 40 | | | |

# Composition

**Objective** _____

| | Target | | | |
|---|---|---|---|---|
| 1 | brick | | | |
| 2 | cloth | | | |
| 3 | glass | | | |
| 4 | leather | | | |
| 5 | metal | | | |
| 6 | plastic | | | |
| 7 | wood | | | |
| 8 | wool | | | |
| 9 | | | | |
| 10 | | | | |

# Computer Game

**Objective** _____

| | Target | | | |
|---|---|---|---|---|
| 1 | Arthur's Reading Race | | | |
| 2 | Bailey's Book House | | | |
| 3 | Blue's ABC Time Activites | | | |
| 4 | D.W. the Picky Eater | | | |
| 5 | Disney's Pocahontas | | | |
| 6 | Disney's Toddler | | | |
| 7 | Just Me and My Mom | | | |
| 8 | My First Incredible Amazing Dictionary | | | |
| 9 | Reader Rabbit 1 | | | |
| 10 | Ready for School Kindergarten | | | |
| 11 | Thomas the Tank Engine | | | |
| 12 | Winnie the Pooh and the Honey Tree | | | |
| 13 | Winnie the Pooh Preschool | | | |
| 14 | | | | |
| 15 | | | | |
| 16 | | | | |
| 17 | | | | |
| 18 | | | | |
| 19 | | | | |
| 20 | | | | |

# Day of the Week

**Objective** _____

| Target | | | |
|---|---|---|---|
| 1 Friday | | | |
| 2 Monday | | | |
| 3 Saturday | | | |
| 4 Sunday | | | |
| 5 Thursday | | | |
| 6 Tuesday | | | |
| 7 Wednesday | | | |

# Electronic

**Objective** _____

| Target | | | |
|---|---|---|---|
| 1 alarm clock | | | |
| 2 calculator | | | |
| 3 camera | | | |
| 4 cassette | | | |
| 5 CD | | | |
| 6 clock | | | |
| 7 computer | | | |
| 8 computer mouse | | | |
| 9 disk | | | |
| 10 dryer | | | |
| 11 DVD | | | |
| 12 fan | | | |
| 13 game boy | | | |
| 14 headphones | | | |
| 15 iron | | | |
| 16 microphone | | | |
| 17 printer | | | |
| 18 radio | | | |
| 19 record | | | |
| 20 record player | | | |
| 21 remote control | | | |
| 22 sewing machine | | | |
| 23 stereo | | | |
| 24 tape recorder | | | |
| 25 TV | | | |

# Electronic

**Objective** _____

| | Target | | | |
|---|---|---|---|---|
| 26 | vacuum | | | |
| 27 | VCR | | | |
| 28 | video | | | |
| 29 | video camera | | | |
| 30 | video game | | | |
| 31 | washing machine | | | |
| 32 | | | | |
| 33 | | | | |
| 34 | | | | |
| 35 | | | | |

# Event

**Objective** _____

| | Target | | | |
|---|---|---|---|---|
| 1 | appointment | | | |
| 2 | barbeque | | | |
| 3 | birthday | | | |
| 4 | breakfast | | | |
| 5 | carnival | | | |
| 6 | concert | | | |
| 7 | dinner | | | |
| 8 | eye exam | | | |
| 9 | fair | | | |
| 10 | lunch | | | |
| 11 | meeting | | | |
| 12 | movie | | | |
| 13 | nap | | | |
| 14 | party | | | |
| 15 | PE | | | |
| 16 | piggyback | | | |
| 17 | play | | | |
| 18 | presentation | | | |
| 19 | recess | | | |
| 20 | rodeo | | | |
| 21 | show | | | |
| 22 | story time | | | |
| 23 | visit | | | |
| 24 | wedding | | | |
| 25 | | | | |

# Fairy Tale

**Objective** _____

| | Target | | | |
|---|---|---|---|---|
| 1 | angel | | | |
| 2 | devil | | | |
| 3 | dragon | | | |
| 4 | dwarf | | | |
| 5 | elf | | | |
| 6 | ghost | | | |
| 7 | giant | | | |
| 8 | king | | | |
| 9 | monster | | | |
| 10 | prince | | | |
| 11 | princess | | | |
| 12 | queen | | | |
| 13 | Santa | | | |
| 14 | witch | | | |
| 15 | wizard | | | |
| 16 | | | | |
| 17 | | | | |
| 18 | | | | |
| 19 | | | | |
| 20 | | | | |
| 21 | | | | |
| 22 | | | | |
| 23 | | | | |
| 24 | | | | |
| 25 | | | | |
| 26 | | | | |
| 27 | | | | |
| 28 | | | | |
| 29 | | | | |
| 30 | | | | |
| 31 | | | | |
| 32 | | | | |
| 33 | | | | |
| 34 | | | | |
| 35 | | | | |
| 36 | | | | |
| 37 | | | | |
| 38 | | | | |
| 39 | | | | |
| 40 | | | | |

# Food

**Objective** _____

| Target | | | |
|---|---|---|---|
| 1 bagel | | | |
| 2 bread | | | |
| 3 bread sticks | | | |
| 4 brown sugar | | | |
| 5 bun | | | |
| 6 butter | | | |
| 7 cereal | | | |
| 8 cereal bar | | | |
| 9 cheese | | | |
| 10 cottage cheese | | | |
| 11 cream of rice | | | |
| 12 crust | | | |
| 13 egg | | | |
| 14 flour | | | |
| 15 french fries | | | |
| 16 french toast | | | |
| 17 fried egg | | | |
| 18 fruit | | | |
| 19 ingredient | | | |
| 20 jelly | | | |
| 21 ketchup | | | |
| 22 macaroni | | | |
| 23 macaroni and cheese | | | |
| 24 mayonnaise | | | |
| 25 meal | | | |
| 26 meat | | | |
| 27 noodles | | | |
| 28 nut | | | |
| 29 oatmeal | | | |
| 30 oil | | | |
| 31 omelet | | | |
| 32 onion rings | | | |
| 33 pancake | | | |
| 34 peanut | | | |
| 35 peanut butter | | | |
| 36 pizza | | | |
| 37 popcorn | | | |
| 38 rice | | | |
| 39 rice cake | | | |
| 40 salad | | | |

# Food

**Objective** _____

| Target | | | |
|---|---|---|---|
| 41 salt | | | |
| 42 sandwich | | | |
| 43 snack | | | |
| 44 soup | | | |
| 45 spaghetti | | | |
| 46 spices | | | |
| 47 sugar | | | |
| 48 syrup | | | |
| 49 toast | | | |
| 50 tomato sauce | | | |
| 51 vegetables | | | |
| 52 waffle | | | |
| 53 yogurt | | | |
| 54 yoke | | | |
| 55 | | | |
| 56 | | | |
| 57 | | | |
| 58 | | | |
| 59 | | | |
| 60 | | | |

# Food ~ Drink

**Objective** _____

| Target | | | |
|---|---|---|---|
| 1 cocoa | | | |
| 2 coffee | | | |
| 3 drink | | | |
| 4 hot chocolate | | | |
| 5 ice | | | |
| 6 juice | | | |
| 7 lemonade | | | |
| 8 milk | | | |
| 9 pop | | | |
| 10 soda | | | |
| 11 tea | | | |
| 12 water | | | |
| 13 wine | | | |

# Food ~ Fruit

**Objective** _____

| | Target | | | |
|---|---|---|---|---|
| 1 | apple | | | |
| 2 | applesauce | | | |
| 3 | banana | | | |
| 4 | blackberry | | | |
| 5 | blueberry | | | |
| 6 | cantaloupe | | | |
| 7 | cherry | | | |
| 8 | grapefruit | | | |
| 9 | grapes | | | |
| 10 | honeydew | | | |
| 11 | kiwi | | | |
| 12 | lemon | | | |
| 13 | lime | | | |
| 14 | nectarine | | | |
| 15 | olive | | | |
| 16 | orange | | | |
| 17 | peach | | | |
| 18 | pear | | | |
| 19 | pineapple | | | |
| 20 | prunes | | | |
| 21 | raisin | | | |
| 22 | raspberry | | | |
| 23 | strawberry | | | |
| 24 | tomato | | | |
| 25 | watermelon | | | |
| 26 | | | | |
| 27 | | | | |
| 28 | | | | |
| 29 | | | | |
| 30 | | | | |
| 31 | | | | |
| 32 | | | | |
| 33 | | | | |
| 34 | | | | |
| 35 | | | | |
| 36 | | | | |
| 37 | | | | |
| 38 | | | | |
| 39 | | | | |
| 40 | | | | |

# Food ~ Meat

**Objective** _____

| | Target | | | |
|---|---|---|---|---|
| 1 | bacon | | | |
| 2 | burger | | | |
| 3 | cheese burger | | | |
| 4 | chicken breast | | | |
| 5 | chicken nuggets | | | |
| 6 | corndog | | | |
| 7 | fish | | | |
| 8 | ham | | | |
| 9 | hamburger | | | |
| 10 | hotdog | | | |
| 11 | salami | | | |
| 12 | sausage | | | |
| 13 | tuna | | | |
| 14 | turkey | | | |
| 15 | | | | |
| 16 | | | | |
| 17 | | | | |
| 18 | | | | |
| 19 | | | | |
| 20 | | | | |

# Food ~ Snack

**Objective** _____

| | Target | | | |
|---|---|---|---|---|
| 1 | chips | | | |
| 2 | cracker | | | |
| 3 | fruit rollup | | | |
| 4 | gum ball | | | |
| 5 | lollipop | | | |
| 6 | pretzel | | | |
| 7 | | | | |
| 8 | | | | |
| 9 | | | | |
| 10 | | | | |
| 11 | | | | |
| 12 | | | | |
| 13 | | | | |
| 14 | | | | |
| 15 | | | | |

# Food ~ Sweets

**Objective** _____

| | Target | | | |
|---|---|---|---|---|
| 1 | brownie | | | |
| 2 | cake | | | |
| 3 | candy | | | |
| 4 | candy bar | | | |
| 5 | candy cane | | | |
| 6 | chocolate | | | |
| 7 | chocolate chips | | | |
| 8 | chocolate syrup | | | |
| 9 | cookie | | | |
| 10 | danish | | | |
| 11 | donut | | | |
| 12 | gingerbread man | | | |
| 13 | honey | | | |
| 14 | ice cream | | | |
| 15 | marshmallow | | | |
| 16 | marshmallow creme | | | |
| 17 | muffin | | | |
| 18 | pie | | | |
| 19 | | | | |
| 20 | | | | |
| 21 | | | | |
| 22 | | | | |
| 23 | | | | |
| 24 | | | | |
| 25 | | | | |
| 26 | | | | |
| 27 | | | | |
| 28 | | | | |
| 29 | | | | |
| 30 | | | | |
| 31 | | | | |
| 32 | | | | |
| 33 | | | | |
| 34 | | | | |
| 35 | | | | |
| 36 | | | | |
| 37 | | | | |
| 38 | | | | |
| 39 | | | | |
| 40 | | | | |

# Food ~ Vegetable

**Objective** _____

| | Target | | | |
|---|---|---|---|---|
| 1 | beans | | | |
| 2 | broccoli | | | |
| 3 | cabbage | | | |
| 4 | carrot | | | |
| 5 | cauliflower | | | |
| 6 | celery | | | |
| 7 | corn | | | |
| 8 | eggplant | | | |
| 9 | green bean | | | |
| 10 | green pepper | | | |
| 11 | lettuce | | | |
| 12 | mushroom | | | |
| 13 | onion | | | |
| 14 | peas | | | |
| 15 | pepper | | | |
| 16 | pickle | | | |
| 17 | potato | | | |
| 18 | pumpkin | | | |
| 19 | radish | | | |
| 20 | red pepper | | | |
| 21 | squash | | | |
| 22 | sweet potato | | | |
| 23 | yellow squash | | | |
| 24 | zucchini | | | |
| 25 | | | | |
| 26 | | | | |
| 27 | | | | |
| 28 | | | | |
| 29 | | | | |
| 30 | | | | |
| 31 | | | | |
| 32 | | | | |
| 33 | | | | |
| 34 | | | | |
| 35 | | | | |
| 36 | | | | |
| 37 | | | | |
| 38 | | | | |
| 39 | | | | |
| 40 | | | | |

# Footwear

**Objective** _____

| | Target | | | |
|---|---|---|---|---|
| 1 | boot | | | |
| 2 | flip flop | | | |
| 3 | flippers | | | |
| 4 | sandal | | | |
| 5 | shoe | | | |
| 6 | slippers | | | |
| 7 | sneaker | | | |
| 8 | sock | | | |
| 9 | | | | |
| 10 | | | | |

# Furniture

**Objective** _____

| | Target | | | |
|---|---|---|---|---|
| 1 | cabinet | | | |
| 2 | chair | | | |
| 3 | couch | | | |
| 4 | desk | | | |
| 5 | door | | | |
| 6 | frame | | | |
| 7 | high chair | | | |
| 8 | lamp | | | |
| 9 | mantle | | | |
| 10 | patio set | | | |
| 11 | playpen | | | |
| 12 | rocking chair | | | |
| 13 | rug | | | |
| 14 | seat | | | |
| 15 | shelf | | | |
| 16 | stool | | | |
| 17 | table | | | |
| 18 | | | | |
| 19 | | | | |
| 20 | | | | |
| 21 | | | | |
| 22 | | | | |
| 23 | | | | |
| 24 | | | | |
| 25 | | | | |

# Game

**Objective** _____

| **Target** | | | |
|---|---|---|---|
| 1 Barnyard Bingo | | | |
| 2 Candyland | | | |
| 3 Chute and Ladders | | | |
| 4 Hide and Seek | | | |
| 5 Hot Potato | | | |
| 6 Lotto | | | |
| 7 Memory | | | |
| 8 Mr. Potato Head | | | |
| 9 Oreo Matching | | | |
| 10 Red Light Green Light | | | |
| 11 Ring Around the Rosie | | | |
| 12 Tic-Tac Tony | | | |
| 13 | | | |
| 14 | | | |
| 15 | | | |
| 16 | | | |
| 17 | | | |
| 18 | | | |
| 19 | | | |
| 20 | | | |

# Holiday

**Objective** _____

| **Target** | | | |
|---|---|---|---|
| 1 Christmas | | | |
| 2 Christmas tree | | | |
| 3 Easter basket | | | |
| 4 Fourth of July | | | |
| 5 Halloween | | | |
| 6 Hanukkah | | | |
| 7 mask | | | |
| 8 present | | | |
| 9 Thanksgiving | | | |
| 10 | | | |
| 11 | | | |
| 12 | | | |
| 13 | | | |
| 14 | | | |

# Household

**Objective** _____

| | Target | | | |
|---|---|---|---|---|
| 1 | aquarium | | | |
| 2 | bag | | | |
| 3 | basket | | | |
| 4 | batteries | | | |
| 5 | bottle | | | |
| 6 | box | | | |
| 7 | clothes pin | | | |
| 8 | detergent | | | |
| 9 | dish liquid | | | |
| 10 | door knob | | | |
| 11 | fish tank | | | |
| 12 | garbage can | | | |
| 13 | ironing board | | | |
| 14 | jar | | | |
| 15 | key | | | |
| 16 | leash | | | |
| 17 | lid | | | |
| 18 | light bulb | | | |
| 19 | light switch | | | |
| 20 | lunch bag | | | |
| 21 | lunch box | | | |
| 22 | measuring tape | | | |
| 23 | newspaper | | | |
| 24 | paper bag | | | |
| 25 | phone book | | | |
| 26 | photo | | | |
| 27 | picture | | | |
| 28 | push pin | | | |
| 29 | smoke detector | | | |
| 30 | telephone | | | |
| 31 | telephone book | | | |
| 32 | ticket | | | |
| 33 | trash can | | | |
| 34 | tray | | | |
| 35 | walkie talkie | | | |
| 36 | waste basket | | | |
| 37 | yarn | | | |
| 38 | | | | |
| 39 | | | | |
| 40 | | | | |

# Instrument

**Objective** _____

| | Target | | | |
|---|---|---|---|---|
| 1 | band | | | |
| 2 | bell | | | |
| 3 | bugle | | | |
| 4 | clarinet | | | |
| 5 | drum | | | |
| 6 | drum sticks | | | |
| 7 | flute | | | |
| 8 | guitar | | | |
| 9 | horn | | | |
| 10 | keyboard | | | |
| 11 | maraca | | | |
| 12 | organ | | | |
| 13 | party horn | | | |
| 14 | piano | | | |
| 15 | recorder | | | |
| 16 | saxophone | | | |
| 17 | tambourine | | | |
| 18 | trombone | | | |
| 19 | trumpet | | | |
| 20 | violin | | | |
| 21 | xylophone | | | |
| 22 | | | | |
| 23 | | | | |
| 24 | | | | |
| 25 | | | | |
| 26 | | | | |
| 27 | | | | |
| 28 | | | | |
| 29 | | | | |
| 30 | | | | |
| 31 | | | | |
| 32 | | | | |
| 33 | | | | |
| 34 | | | | |
| 35 | | | | |
| 36 | | | | |
| 37 | | | | |
| 38 | | | | |
| 39 | | | | |
| 40 | | | | |

# Kitchen

**Objective** _____

| | Target | | | |
|---|---|---|---|---|
| 1 | blender | | | |
| 2 | bowl | | | |
| 3 | can opener | | | |
| 4 | candle | | | |
| 5 | container | | | |
| 6 | cookie sheet | | | |
| 7 | counter | | | |
| 8 | cup | | | |
| 9 | cupboard | | | |
| 10 | dishes | | | |
| 11 | dishwasher | | | |
| 12 | drawer | | | |
| 13 | foil | | | |
| 14 | fork | | | |
| 15 | grater | | | |
| 16 | groceries | | | |
| 17 | knife | | | |
| 18 | ladle | | | |
| 19 | measuring cup | | | |
| 20 | measuring spoon | | | |
| 21 | microwave | | | |
| 22 | mixer | | | |
| 23 | muffin tin | | | |
| 24 | mug | | | |
| 25 | napkin | | | |
| 26 | oven | | | |
| 27 | pan | | | |
| 28 | paper towel | | | |
| 29 | pitcher | | | |
| 30 | placemat | | | |
| 31 | plastic bag | | | |
| 32 | plastic wrap | | | |
| 33 | plate | | | |
| 34 | plug | | | |
| 35 | pot | | | |
| 36 | rag | | | |
| 37 | refrigerator | | | |
| 38 | rolling pin | | | |
| 39 | scraper | | | |
| 40 | scrubber | | | |

# Kitchen

**Objective** _____

| Target | | | |
|---|---|---|---|
| 41 sharp knife | | | |
| 42 silverware | | | |
| 43 sponge | | | |
| 44 spoon | | | |
| 45 stove | | | |
| 46 strainer | | | |
| 47 straw | | | |
| 48 table cloth | | | |
| 49 teapot | | | |
| 50 timer | | | |
| 51 toaster oven | | | |
| 52 tongs | | | |
| 53 toothpick | | | |
| 54 vase | | | |
| 55 | | | |
| 56 | | | |
| 57 | | | |
| 58 | | | |
| 59 | | | |
| 60 | | | |
| 61 | | | |
| 62 | | | |
| 63 | | | |
| 64 | | | |
| 65 | | | |

# Land Form

**Objective** _____

| Target | | | |
|---|---|---|---|
| 1 canyon | | | |
| 2 cliff | | | |
| 3 desert | | | |
| 4 field | | | |
| 5 glacier | | | |
| 6 hill | | | |
| 7 iceberg | | | |
| 8 island | | | |
| 9 mountain | | | |
| 10 valley | | | |
| 11 volcano | | | |

# Letter

**Objective** _____

| | Target | | | |
|---|---|---|---|---|
| 1 | A | | | |
| 2 | B | | | |
| 3 | C | | | |
| 4 | D | | | |
| 5 | E | | | |
| 6 | F | | | |
| 7 | G | | | |
| 8 | H | | | |
| 9 | I | | | |
| 10 | J | | | |
| 11 | K | | | |
| 12 | L | | | |
| 13 | M | | | |
| 14 | N | | | |
| 15 | O | | | |
| 16 | P | | | |
| 17 | Q | | | |
| 18 | R | | | |
| 19 | S | | | |
| 20 | T | | | |
| 21 | U | | | |
| 22 | V | | | |
| 23 | W | | | |
| 24 | X | | | |
| 25 | Y | | | |
| 26 | Z | | | |

# Math

**Objective** _____

| | Target | | | |
|---|---|---|---|---|
| 1 | add | | | |
| 2 | equals | | | |
| 3 | line | | | |
| 4 | minus | | | |
| 5 | plus | | | |
| 6 | subtract | | | |
| 7 | take away | | | |
| 8 | | | | |
| 9 | | | | |

# Miscellaneous Noun

**Objective** _____

| | Target | | | |
|---|---|---|---|---|
| 1 | address | | | |
| 2 | age | | | |
| 3 | check box | | | |
| 4 | comma | | | |
| 5 | credit card | | | |
| 6 | dot | | | |
| 7 | end | | | |
| 8 | exclamation point | | | |
| 9 | fun | | | |
| 10 | gift | | | |
| 11 | kind | | | |
| 12 | knot | | | |
| 13 | matter | | | |
| 14 | maze | | | |
| 15 | mess | | | |
| 16 | name | | | |
| 17 | noise | | | |
| 18 | paragraph | | | |
| 19 | period | | | |
| 20 | question | | | |
| 21 | question mark | | | |
| 22 | rear | | | |
| 23 | receipt | | | |
| 24 | sentence | | | |
| 25 | song | | | |
| 26 | spot | | | |
| 27 | trick | | | |
| 28 | trouble | | | |
| 29 | way | | | |
| 30 | word | | | |
| 31 | | | | |
| 32 | | | | |
| 33 | | | | |
| 34 | | | | |
| 35 | | | | |
| 36 | | | | |
| 37 | | | | |
| 38 | | | | |
| 39 | | | | |
| 40 | | | | |

# Money

**Objective** _____

| | Target | | | |
|---|---|---|---|---|
| 1 | cash register | | | |
| 2 | coupon | | | |
| 3 | dime | | | |
| 4 | dollar | | | |
| 5 | half dollar | | | |
| 6 | money | | | |
| 7 | nickle | | | |
| 8 | penny | | | |
| 9 | quarter | | | |
| 10 | | | | |
| 11 | | | | |
| 12 | | | | |
| 13 | | | | |
| 14 | | | | |
| 15 | | | | |

# Month

**Objective** _____

| | Target | | | |
|---|---|---|---|---|
| 1 | April | | | |
| 2 | August | | | |
| 3 | December | | | |
| 4 | February | | | |
| 5 | January | | | |
| 6 | July | | | |
| 7 | June | | | |
| 8 | March | | | |
| 9 | May | | | |
| 10 | November | | | |
| 11 | October | | | |
| 12 | September | | | |
| 13 | | | | |
| 14 | | | | |
| 15 | | | | |

# Nature

**Objective** _____

| Target | | | |
|---|---|---|---|
| 1 acorn | | | |
| 2 cactus | | | |
| 3 clover | | | |
| 4 coral | | | |
| 5 dirt | | | |
| 6 fire | | | |
| 7 flower | | | |
| 8 fountain | | | |
| 9 garden | | | |
| 10 grass | | | |
| 11 hay | | | |
| 12 heat | | | |
| 13 icicle | | | |
| 14 leaf | | | |
| 15 log | | | |
| 16 mud | | | |
| 17 nest | | | |
| 18 orchard | | | |
| 19 palm tree | | | |
| 20 pinecone | | | |
| 21 plant | | | |
| 22 rock | | | |
| 23 sand | | | |
| 24 seashell | | | |
| 25 shadow | | | |
| 26 sky | | | |
| 27 smoke | | | |
| 28 space | | | |
| 29 spider web | | | |
| 30 stick | | | |
| 31 stones | | | |
| 32 sunrise | | | |
| 33 sunset | | | |
| 34 tree | | | |
| 35 world | | | |
| 36 | | | |
| 37 | | | |
| 38 | | | |
| 39 | | | |
| 40 | | | |

# Number

**Objective** _____

| Target | | | |
|---|---|---|---|
| 1 eight | | | |
| 2 eighteen | | | |
| 3 eighth | | | |
| 4 eleven | | | |
| 5 fifteen | | | |
| 6 fifth | | | |
| 7 first | | | |
| 8 five | | | |
| 9 four | | | |
| 10 fourteen | | | |
| 11 fourth | | | |
| 12 hundred | | | |
| 13 nine | | | |
| 14 nineteen | | | |
| 15 ninth | | | |
| 16 one | | | |
| 17 second | | | |
| 18 seven | | | |
| 19 seventeen | | | |
| 20 seventh | | | |
| 21 six | | | |
| 22 sixteen | | | |
| 23 sixth | | | |
| 24 ten | | | |
| 25 tenth | | | |
| 26 third | | | |
| 27 thirteen | | | |
| 28 three | | | |
| 29 twelve | | | |
| 30 twenty | | | |
| 31 two | | | |
| 32 zero | | | |
| 33 | | | |
| 34 | | | |
| 35 | | | |
| 36 | | | |
| 37 | | | |
| 38 | | | |
| 39 | | | |
| 40 | | | |

# Outside

**Objective** _____

| Target | | | |
|---|---|---|---|
| 1 air | | | |
| 2 ATM | | | |
| 3 cross | | | |
| 4 crosswalk | | | |
| 5 doghouse | | | |
| 6 fire hydrant | | | |
| 7 fireworks | | | |
| 8 flag | | | |
| 9 float | | | |
| 10 foot print | | | |
| 11 gas | | | |
| 12 gas pump | | | |
| 13 grill | | | |
| 14 ground | | | |
| 15 heaven | | | |
| 16 hive | | | |
| 17 hole | | | |
| 18 hut | | | |
| 19 lantern | | | |
| 20 lawn | | | |
| 21 litter | | | |
| 22 mailbox | | | |
| 23 parade | | | |
| 24 pole | | | |
| 25 post | | | |
| 26 saddle | | | |
| 27 sidewalk | | | |
| 28 sleeping bag | | | |
| 29 snowman | | | |
| 30 teepee | | | |
| 31 tent | | | |
| 32 traffic | | | |
| 33 traffic light | | | |
| 34 USA flag | | | |
| 35 woods | | | |
| 36 | | | |
| 37 | | | |
| 38 | | | |
| 39 | | | |
| 40 | | | |

# Person

**Objective** _____

| Target | | | |
|---|---|---|---|
| 1 adult | | | |
| 2 artist | | | |
| 3 athlete | | | |
| 4 aunt | | | |
| 5 author | | | |
| 6 baby | | | |
| 7 babysitter | | | |
| 8 baseball player | | | |
| 9 basketball player | | | |
| 10 boy | | | |
| 11 boy scout | | | |
| 12 bride | | | |
| 13 brother | | | |
| 14 brownie | | | |
| 15 cheer leader | | | |
| 16 child | | | |
| 17 children | | | |
| 18 clown | | | |
| 19 conductor | | | |
| 20 cowboy | | | |
| 21 dad | | | |
| 22 dancer | | | |
| 23 Eskimo | | | |
| 24 father | | | |
| 25 fisherman | | | |
| 26 football player | | | |
| 27 friend | | | |
| 28 friends | | | |
| 29 girl | | | |
| 30 girl scout | | | |
| 31 graduate | | | |
| 32 grandma | | | |
| 33 grandpa | | | |
| 34 groom | | | |
| 35 gypsy | | | |
| 36 husband | | | |
| 37 illustrator | | | |
| 38 Indian | | | |
| 39 jockey | | | |
| 40 kid | | | |

Language Targets to Teach a Child to Communicate

# Person

**Objective** _____

| | Target | | | |
|---|---|---|---|---|
| 41 | king | | | |
| 42 | knight | | | |
| 43 | lady | | | |
| 44 | magician | | | |
| 45 | man | | | |
| 46 | mom | | | |
| 47 | mother | | | |
| 48 | musician | | | |
| 49 | neighbor | | | |
| 50 | parent | | | |
| 51 | passenger | | | |
| 52 | person | | | |
| 53 | photographer | | | |
| 54 | reporter | | | |
| 55 | sailor | | | |
| 56 | scientist | | | |
| 57 | sister | | | |
| 58 | soccer player | | | |
| 59 | tennis player | | | |
| 60 | truck driver | | | |
| 61 | uncle | | | |
| 62 | wife | | | |
| 63 | woman | | | |
| 64 | | | | |
| 65 | | | | |
| 66 | | | | |
| 67 | | | | |
| 68 | | | | |
| 69 | | | | |
| 70 | | | | |
| 71 | | | | |
| 72 | | | | |
| 73 | | | | |
| 74 | | | | |
| 75 | | | | |
| 76 | | | | |
| 77 | | | | |
| 78 | | | | |
| 79 | | | | |
| 80 | | | | |

# Place

**Objective** _____

| | Target | | | |
|---|---|---|---|---|
| 1 | airport | | | |
| 2 | animal hospital | | | |
| 3 | backyard | | | |
| 4 | ball pit | | | |
| 5 | bank | | | |
| 6 | barn | | | |
| 7 | Barnes and Noble | | | |
| 8 | beach | | | |
| 9 | Blockbusters | | | |
| 10 | building | | | |
| 11 | cabin | | | |
| 12 | camp | | | |
| 13 | car wash | | | |
| 14 | castle | | | |
| 15 | cave | | | |
| 16 | cemetery | | | |
| 17 | church | | | |
| 18 | city | | | |
| 19 | Disneyland | | | |
| 20 | downstairs | | | |
| 21 | drive thru | | | |
| 22 | dump | | | |
| 23 | farm | | | |
| 24 | fire station | | | |
| 25 | forest | | | |
| 26 | gas station | | | |
| 27 | grocery store | | | |
| 28 | harbor | | | |
| 29 | home | | | |
| 30 | hospital | | | |
| 31 | hotel | | | |
| 32 | house | | | |
| 33 | igloo | | | |
| 34 | indoor play area | | | |
| 35 | jungle | | | |
| 36 | Kinkos | | | |
| 37 | library | | | |
| 38 | light house | | | |
| 39 | mall | | | |
| 40 | motel | | | |

# Place

**Objective** _____

| Target | | | |
|---|---|---|---|
| 41 movies | | | |
| 42 museum | | | |
| 43 Office Depot | | | |
| 44 park | | | |
| 45 path | | | |
| 46 Payless Shoe Source | | | |
| 47 playground | | | |
| 48 police station | | | |
| 49 pool | | | |
| 50 porch | | | |
| 51 post office | | | |
| 52 ranch | | | |
| 53 restaurant | | | |
| 54 Rite Aid | | | |
| 55 runway | | | |
| 56 Safeway | | | |
| 57 shed | | | |
| 58 sky scraper | | | |
| 59 Space Needle | | | |
| 60 store | | | |
| 61 Supercuts | | | |
| 62 synagogue | | | |
| 63 Target | | | |
| 64 tennis court | | | |
| 65 theater | | | |
| 66 town | | | |
| 67 town hall | | | |
| 68 toy store | | | |
| 69 train station | | | |
| 70 upstairs | | | |
| 71 waiting room | | | |
| 72 Wal-Mart | | | |
| 73 water tower | | | |
| 74 windmill | | | |
| 75 zoo | | | |
| 76 | | | |
| 77 | | | |
| 78 | | | |
| 79 | | | |
| 80 | | | |

# Playground

**Objective** _____

| | Target | | | |
|---|---|---|---|---|
| 1 | bench | | | |
| 2 | bouncy | | | |
| 3 | merry go round | | | |
| 4 | monkey bars | | | |
| 5 | picnic table | | | |
| 6 | sandbox | | | |
| 7 | see saw | | | |
| 8 | slide | | | |
| 9 | swing | | | |
| 10 | teeter totter | | | |
| 11 | tire swing | | | |
| 12 | | | | |
| 13 | | | | |
| 14 | | | | |
| 15 | | | | |

# Religion

**Objective** _____

| | Target | | | |
|---|---|---|---|---|
| 1 | Bible | | | |
| 2 | Buddha | | | |
| 3 | Crucifix | | | |
| 4 | Jesus Christ | | | |
| 5 | Menorah | | | |
| 6 | Star of David | | | |
| 7 | | | | |
| 8 | | | | |
| 9 | | | | |
| 10 | | | | |
| 11 | | | | |
| 12 | | | | |
| 13 | | | | |
| 14 | | | | |
| 15 | | | | |

# Restaurant

**Objective** _____

| Target | | | |
|---|---|---|---|
| 1 Applebees | | | |
| 2 Burger King | | | |
| 3 Chilis | | | |
| 4 FatBurger | | | |
| 5 KFC | | | |
| 6 Krispy Kreme | | | |
| 7 McDonalds | | | |
| 8 Pizza Hut | | | |
| 9 Starbucks | | | |
| 10 Taco Bell | | | |
| 11 Wendys | | | |
| 12 | | | |
| 13 | | | |
| 14 | | | |
| 15 | | | |

# Room

**Objective** _____

| Target | | | |
|---|---|---|---|
| 1 basement | | | |
| 2 bathroom | | | |
| 3 bedroom | | | |
| 4 carpet | | | |
| 5 ceiling | | | |
| 6 corner | | | |
| 7 den | | | |
| 8 dining room | | | |
| 9 family room | | | |
| 10 floor | | | |
| 11 foyer | | | |
| 12 garage | | | |
| 13 hall way | | | |
| 14 kitchen | | | |
| 15 laundry room | | | |
| 16 living room | | | |
| 17 office | | | |
| 18 pantry | | | |
| 19 play room | | | |
| 20 wall | | | |

# School

**Objective** _____

| | Target | | | |
|---|---|---|---|---|
| 1 | backpack | | | |
| 2 | book | | | |
| 3 | calculator | | | |
| 4 | calendar | | | |
| 5 | cartoon | | | |
| 6 | chalk | | | |
| 7 | chalk board | | | |
| 8 | classroom | | | |
| 9 | coat hook | | | |
| 10 | crayon | | | |
| 11 | cubby | | | |
| 12 | easel | | | |
| 13 | envelope | | | |
| 14 | eraser | | | |
| 15 | globe | | | |
| 16 | glue | | | |
| 17 | Kindergarten | | | |
| 18 | locker | | | |
| 19 | magazine | | | |
| 20 | mail | | | |
| 21 | marker | | | |
| 22 | notebook | | | |
| 23 | pad | | | |
| 24 | page | | | |
| 25 | paintbrush | | | |
| 26 | paper | | | |
| 27 | paper clip | | | |
| 28 | pen | | | |
| 29 | pencil | | | |
| 30 | pencil sharpener | | | |
| 31 | ruler | | | |
| 32 | schedule | | | |
| 33 | school | | | |
| 34 | scissors | | | |
| 35 | stapler | | | |
| 36 | story | | | |
| 37 | tape | | | |
| 38 | | | | |
| 39 | | | | |
| 40 | | | | |

# Season

**Objective** _____

| **Target** | | | |
|---|---|---|---|
| 1 autumn | | | |
| 2 spring | | | |
| 3 summer | | | |
| 4 winter | | | |

# Shape

**Objective** _____

| **Target** | | | |
|---|---|---|---|
| 1 circle | | | |
| 2 diamond | | | |
| 3 heart | | | |
| 4 hexagon | | | |
| 5 octagon | | | |
| 6 oval | | | |
| 7 rectangle | | | |
| 8 square | | | |
| 9 star | | | |
| 10 trapezoid | | | |
| 11 triangle | | | |
| 12 | | | |
| 13 | | | |

# Sick

**Objective** _____

| **Target** | | | |
|---|---|---|---|
| 1 aspirin | | | |
| 2 bandage | | | |
| 3 bandaid | | | |
| 4 boo boo | | | |
| 5 bruise | | | |
| 6 bump | | | |
| 7 dropper | | | |
| 8 medicine | | | |
| 9 shot | | | |
| 10 thermometer | | | |
| 11 xray | | | |

# Sign

**Objective** _____

| Target | | | |
|---|---|---|---|
| 1  do not enter | | | |
| 2  exit | | | |
| 3  hospital sign | | | |
| 4  library sign | | | |
| 5  school sign | | | |
| 6  stop sign | | | |
| 7 | | | |
| 8 | | | |
| 9 | | | |
| 10 | | | |
| 11 | | | |
| 12 | | | |
| 13 | | | |
| 14 | | | |
| 15 | | | |

# Space

**Objective** _____

| Target | | | |
|---|---|---|---|
| 1  astronaut | | | |
| 2  earth | | | |
| 3  moon | | | |
| 4  planet | | | |
| 5  satellite | | | |
| 6  space helmet | | | |
| 7  space mission | | | |
| 8  space ship | | | |
| 9  space shuttle | | | |
| 10  space suit | | | |
| 11  star | | | |
| 12  sun | | | |
| 13  telescope | | | |
| 14 | | | |
| 15 | | | |
| 16 | | | |
| 17 | | | |
| 18 | | | |
| 19 | | | |
| 20 | | | |

# Sport

**Objective** _____

| Target | | | |
|---|---|---|---|
| 1  base | | | |
| 2  baseball | | | |
| 3  baseball field | | | |
| 4  basketball | | | |
| 5  bat | | | |
| 6  bow and arrow | | | |
| 7  diving board | | | |
| 8  elbow pad | | | |
| 9  fins | | | |
| 10  fishing pole | | | |
| 11  football | | | |
| 12  frisbee | | | |
| 13  glove | | | |
| 14  golf | | | |
| 15  hiker | | | |
| 16  hockey player | | | |
| 17  horse shoe | | | |
| 18  ice skates | | | |
| 19  kneepad | | | |
| 20  paddle | | | |
| 21  parasailing | | | |
| 22  roller blades | | | |
| 23  skate | | | |
| 24  skateboard | | | |
| 25  skis | | | |
| 26  skydiver | | | |
| 27  sled | | | |
| 28  snow shoes | | | |
| 29  soccer ball | | | |
| 30  somersault | | | |
| 31  squash | | | |
| 32  surfboard | | | |
| 33  t-ball | | | |
| 34  team | | | |
| 35  tennis racquet | | | |
| 36  trampoline | | | |
| 37  trophy | | | |
| 38  umpire | | | |
| 39  volley ball | | | |
| 40  wrist guard | | | |

# Structure

**Objective** _____

| | Target | | | |
|---|---|---|---|---|
| 1 | bridge | | | |
| 2 | chimney | | | |
| 3 | dumpster | | | |
| 4 | elevator | | | |
| 5 | escalator | | | |
| 6 | fence | | | |
| 7 | fire escape | | | |
| 8 | fire place | | | |
| 9 | gate | | | |
| 10 | lock | | | |
| 11 | roof | | | |
| 12 | side | | | |
| 13 | socket | | | |
| 14 | stairs | | | |
| 15 | steps | | | |
| 16 | window | | | |
| 17 | | | | |
| 18 | | | | |
| 19 | | | | |
| 20 | | | | |

# Stuff

**Objective** _____

| | Target | | | |
|---|---|---|---|---|
| 1 | dodad | | | |
| 2 | junk | | | |
| 3 | stuff | | | |
| 4 | thing | | | |
| 5 | | | | |
| 6 | | | | |
| 7 | | | | |
| 8 | | | | |
| 9 | | | | |
| 10 | | | | |
| 11 | | | | |
| 12 | | | | |
| 13 | | | | |
| 14 | | | | |
| 15 | | | | |

# Tool

**Objective** _____

| | **Target** | | | |
|---|---|---|---|---|
| 1 | broom | | | |
| 2 | cart | | | |
| 3 | chain | | | |
| 4 | chainsaw | | | |
| 5 | drill | | | |
| 6 | dustpan | | | |
| 7 | fire extinguisher | | | |
| 8 | flashlight | | | |
| 9 | gun | | | |
| 10 | hammer | | | |
| 11 | hoe | | | |
| 12 | hose | | | |
| 13 | ladder | | | |
| 14 | lawnmower | | | |
| 15 | mop | | | |
| 16 | nail | | | |
| 17 | net | | | |
| 18 | nut | | | |
| 19 | pipe | | | |
| 20 | pliers | | | |
| 21 | rake | | | |
| 22 | roller | | | |
| 23 | rope | | | |
| 24 | saw | | | |
| 25 | screw | | | |
| 26 | screw driver | | | |
| 27 | shovel | | | |
| 28 | string | | | |
| 29 | thimble | | | |
| 30 | thread | | | |
| 31 | watering can | | | |
| 32 | wrench | | | |
| 33 | | | | |
| 34 | | | | |
| 35 | | | | |
| 36 | | | | |
| 37 | | | | |
| 38 | | | | |
| 39 | | | | |
| 40 | | | | |

# Toy

**Objective** _____

| Target | | | |
|---|---|---|---|
| 1 Arthur | | | |
| 2 ball | | | |
| 3 balloon | | | |
| 4 Barbie | | | |
| 5 bear | | | |
| 6 Bert | | | |
| 7 blocks | | | |
| 8 bubbles | | | |
| 9 castle | | | |
| 10 clay | | | |
| 11 clock | | | |
| 12 Cookie Monster | | | |
| 13 doll | | | |
| 14 doll house | | | |
| 15 doodle board | | | |
| 16 Eeorye | | | |
| 17 felt people | | | |
| 18 fire station | | | |
| 19 fire truck | | | |
| 20 game | | | |
| 21 gameboy | | | |
| 22 garage | | | |
| 23 hoop | | | |
| 24 jump rope | | | |
| 25 kazoo | | | |
| 26 kite | | | |
| 27 koosh balls | | | |
| 28 legos | | | |
| 29 lincoln logs | | | |
| 30 Lion King | | | |
| 31 magnets | | | |
| 32 marbles | | | |
| 33 Mickey Mouse | | | |
| 34 Monsters | | | |
| 35 Oscar | | | |
| 36 paints | | | |
| 37 pirate ship | | | |
| 38 playdoh | | | |
| 39 playhouse | | | |
| 40 Pooh | | | |

# Toy

**Objective** _____

| | Target | | | |
|---|---|---|---|---|
| 41 | power rangers | | | |
| 42 | puzzle | | | |
| 43 | roller coaster | | | |
| 44 | shape sorter | | | |
| 45 | stack beads | | | |
| 46 | stencil | | | |
| 47 | sticker | | | |
| 48 | Tarzan | | | |
| 49 | teletubbies | | | |
| 50 | Tigger | | | |
| 51 | tinker toys | | | |
| 52 | toy piano | | | |
| 53 | train track | | | |
| 54 | trains | | | |
| 55 | tricycle | | | |
| 56 | tunnel | | | |
| 57 | view master | | | |
| 58 | Woody | | | |
| 59 | workbench | | | |
| 60 | zoober zots | | | |
| 61 | | | | |
| 62 | | | | |
| 63 | | | | |
| 64 | | | | |
| 65 | | | | |
| 66 | | | | |
| 67 | | | | |
| 68 | | | | |

# Travel

**Objective** _____

| | Target | | | |
|---|---|---|---|---|
| 1 | car seat | | | |
| 2 | luggage | | | |
| 3 | map | | | |
| 4 | railroad tracks | | | |
| 5 | road | | | |
| 6 | seatbelt | | | |
| 7 | suitcase | | | |

# Vehicle

**Objective** _____

| | Target | | | |
|---|---|---|---|---|
| 1 | ambulance | | | |
| 2 | bike | | | |
| 3 | bulldozer | | | |
| 4 | bus | | | |
| 5 | camper | | | |
| 6 | car | | | |
| 7 | carriage | | | |
| 8 | cement mixer | | | |
| 9 | digger | | | |
| 10 | dump truck | | | |
| 11 | fire truck | | | |
| 12 | garbage truck | | | |
| 13 | golf cart | | | |
| 14 | jeep | | | |
| 15 | motorcycle | | | |
| 16 | police motorcycle | | | |
| 17 | sheriff car | | | |
| 18 | shopping cart | | | |
| 19 | sleigh | | | |
| 20 | snow plow | | | |
| 21 | stagecoach | | | |
| 22 | stroller | | | |
| 23 | SUV | | | |
| 24 | tank | | | |
| 25 | taxi | | | |
| 26 | tow truck | | | |
| 27 | tractor | | | |
| 28 | train | | | |
| 29 | trolley | | | |
| 30 | truck | | | |
| 31 | van | | | |
| 32 | wagon | | | |
| 33 | wheel | | | |
| 34 | wheelchair | | | |
| 35 | | | | |
| 36 | | | | |
| 37 | | | | |
| 38 | | | | |
| 39 | | | | |
| 40 | | | | |

# Video

**Objective** _____

| | Target | | | |
|---|---|---|---|---|
| 1 | 101 Dalmatians | | | |
| 2 | Aladdin | | | |
| 3 | Alice in Wonderland | | | |
| 4 | Bambi | | | |
| 5 | Brother Bear | | | |
| 6 | Buzz Lightyear of Star Command | | | |
| 7 | Dinosaur | | | |
| 8 | Dumbo | | | |
| 9 | El Dorado | | | |
| 10 | Finding Nemo | | | |
| 11 | Hercules | | | |
| 12 | Hunchback of Notre Dame | | | |
| 13 | Lady and the Tramp | | | |
| 14 | Lady and the Tramp II | | | |
| 15 | Lion King | | | |
| 16 | Lion King II | | | |
| 17 | Little Mermaid | | | |
| 18 | Mickey's Magical Christmas | | | |
| 19 | Monsters Inc. | | | |
| 20 | Mulan | | | |
| 21 | Peter Pan | | | |
| 22 | Pocahontas | | | |
| 23 | Pooh's Grand Adventure | | | |
| 24 | Robin Hood | | | |
| 25 | Snow White | | | |
| 26 | The Sword in the Stone | | | |
| 27 | Tigger Movie | | | |
| 28 | Toy Story | | | |
| 29 | Toy Story 2 | | | |
| 31 | | | | |
| 32 | | | | |
| 33 | | | | |
| 34 | | | | |
| 35 | | | | |
| 36 | | | | |
| 37 | | | | |
| 38 | | | | |
| 39 | | | | |
| 40 | | | | |

# Weather

**Objective** _____

| Target | | | |
|---|---|---|---|
| 1 clear | | | |
| 2 cloud | | | |
| 3 cloudy | | | |
| 4 cool | | | |
| 5 dew | | | |
| 6 drizzle | | | |
| 7 flood | | | |
| 8 fog | | | |
| 9 freezing | | | |
| 10 frost | | | |
| 11 hail | | | |
| 12 hot | | | |
| 13 hurricane | | | |
| 14 ice | | | |
| 15 lightning | | | |
| 16 puddle | | | |
| 17 rainbow | | | |
| 18 snow | | | |
| 19 snowflake | | | |
| 20 sprinkle | | | |
| 21 storm | | | |
| 22 sunshine | | | |
| 23 temperature | | | |
| 24 thunder | | | |
| 25 tornado | | | |
| 26 warm | | | |
| 27 windy | | | |
| 28 | | | |
| 29 | | | |
| 30 | | | |
| 31 | | | |
| 32 | | | |
| 33 | | | |
| 34 | | | |
| 35 | | | |
| 36 | | | |
| 37 | | | |
| 38 | | | |
| 39 | | | |
| 40 | | | |

# Chapter 2 - Verb

## Verb ~ Set 1

**Objective** _____

| | Target | | | |
|---|---|---|---|---|
| 1 | bake | | | |
| 2 | bark | | | |
| 3 | blink | | | |
| 4 | blow | | | |
| 5 | bounce | | | |
| 6 | break | | | |
| 7 | bring | | | |
| 8 | brush | | | |
| 9 | build | | | |
| 10 | button | | | |
| 11 | buy | | | |
| 12 | carry | | | |
| 13 | catch | | | |
| 14 | chase | | | |
| 15 | clap | | | |
| 16 | clean | | | |
| 17 | climb | | | |
| 18 | close | | | |
| 19 | color | | | |
| 20 | comb | | | |
| 21 | come | | | |
| 22 | cook | | | |
| 23 | cough | | | |
| 24 | count | | | |
| 25 | cover | | | |
| 26 | crash | | | |
| 27 | crawl | | | |
| 28 | cry | | | |
| 29 | cut | | | |
| 30 | dance | | | |
| 31 | dig | | | |
| 32 | draw | | | |
| 33 | dress | | | |
| 34 | drink | | | |
| 35 | drive | | | |
| 36 | dry | | | |
| 37 | eat | | | |
| 38 | fly | | | |
| 39 | go | | | |
| 40 | help | | | |

# Verb ~ Set 1

**Objective** _____

| Target | | | |
|---|---|---|---|
| 41  hit | | | |
| 42  hop | | | |
| 43  hug | | | |
| 44  jump | | | |
| 45  kick | | | |
| 46  kiss | | | |
| 47  knock | | | |
| 48  laugh | | | |
| 49  match | | | |
| 50  move | | | |
| 51  open | | | |
| 52  paint | | | |
| 53  pee | | | |
| 54  play | | | |
| 55  point | | | |
| 56  poop | | | |
| 57  pour | | | |
| 58  pull | | | |
| 59  push | | | |
| 60  read | | | |
| 61  ride | | | |
| 62  run | | | |
| 63  see | | | |
| 64  sing | | | |
| 65  sit | | | |
| 66  sleep | | | |
| 67  slide | | | |
| 68  sneeze | | | |
| 69  spill | | | |
| 70  stand | | | |
| 71  stomp | | | |
| 72  sweep | | | |
| 73  swim | | | |
| 74  swing | | | |
| 75  throw | | | |
| 76  tickle | | | |
| 77  walk | | | |
| 78  want | | | |
| 79  wash | | | |
| 80  wave | | | |

# Verb ~ Set 2

**Objective** _____

| | Target | | | |
|---|---|---|---|---|
| 1 | act | | | |
| 2 | ask | | | |
| 3 | bat | | | |
| 4 | beat | | | |
| 5 | bite | | | |
| 6 | burn | | | |
| 7 | burp | | | |
| 8 | change | | | |
| 9 | chop | | | |
| 10 | dive | | | |
| 11 | drop | | | |
| 12 | dump | | | |
| 13 | erase | | | |
| 14 | excuse | | | |
| 15 | fall | | | |
| 16 | feed | | | |
| 17 | find | | | |
| 18 | finish | | | |
| 19 | fish | | | |
| 20 | fit | | | |
| 21 | fix | | | |
| 22 | float | | | |
| 23 | flush | | | |
| 24 | fold | | | |
| 25 | follow | | | |
| 26 | get | | | |
| 27 | give | | | |
| 28 | hand | | | |
| 29 | have | | | |
| 30 | hear | | | |
| 31 | hide | | | |
| 32 | hold | | | |
| 33 | iron | | | |
| 34 | itch | | | |
| 35 | juggle | | | |
| 36 | keep | | | |
| 37 | like | | | |
| 38 | listen | | | |
| 39 | live | | | |
| 40 | look | | | |

# Verb ~ Set 2

**Objective** _____

| **Target** | | | |
|---|---|---|---|
| 41 love | | | |
| 42 make | | | |
| 43 mix | | | |
| 44 mow | | | |
| 45 name | | | |
| 46 order | | | |
| 47 pat | | | |
| 48 pedal | | | |
| 49 peel | | | |
| 50 pet | | | |
| 51 pick | | | |
| 52 pinch | | | |
| 53 pound | | | |
| 54 pretend | | | |
| 55 put | | | |
| 56 quit | | | |
| 57 race | | | |
| 58 rain | | | |
| 59 rip | | | |
| 60 roll | | | |
| 61 say | | | |
| 62 scratch | | | |
| 63 scrub | | | |
| 64 shake | | | |
| 65 shave | | | |
| 66 shovel | | | |
| 67 sip | | | |
| 68 skate | | | |
| 69 smell | | | |
| 70 smile | | | |
| 71 splash | | | |
| 72 stop | | | |
| 73 touch | | | |
| 74 try | | | |
| 75 wipe | | | |
| 76 work | | | |
| 77 wrestle | | | |
| 78 write | | | |
| 79 yawn | | | |
| 80 zip | | | |

# Verb ~ Set 3

**Objective** _____

| | Target | | | |
|---|---|---|---|---|
| 1 | add | | | |
| 2 | belong | | | |
| 3 | bend | | | |
| 4 | bleed | | | |
| 5 | can | | | |
| 6 | charge | | | |
| 7 | check | | | |
| 8 | chew | | | |
| 9 | choke | | | |
| 10 | cool | | | |
| 11 | crack | | | |
| 12 | deliver | | | |
| 13 | dial | | | |
| 14 | dunk | | | |
| 15 | exercise | | | |
| 16 | feel | | | |
| 17 | fight | | | |
| 18 | fill | | | |
| 19 | hang | | | |
| 20 | kneel | | | |
| 21 | leave | | | |
| 22 | lick | | | |
| 23 | lie | | | |
| 24 | lock | | | |
| 25 | march | | | |
| 26 | mark | | | |
| 27 | mop | | | |
| 28 | paddle | | | |
| 29 | plug | | | |
| 30 | pop | | | |
| 31 | pump | | | |
| 32 | punch | | | |
| 33 | reach | | | |
| 34 | rest | | | |
| 35 | ring | | | |
| 36 | roast | | | |
| 37 | rock | | | |
| 38 | scream | | | |
| 39 | set | | | |
| 40 | sew | | | |

# Verb ~ Set 3

**Objective** _____

| | Target | | | |
|---|---|---|---|---|
| 41 | share | | | |
| 42 | shine | | | |
| 43 | shoot | | | |
| 44 | shop | | | |
| 45 | show | | | |
| 46 | shut | | | |
| 47 | slip | | | |
| 48 | snap | | | |
| 49 | snore | | | |
| 50 | snow | | | |
| 51 | snuggle | | | |
| 52 | spell | | | |
| 53 | spin | | | |
| 54 | spit | | | |
| 55 | spray | | | |
| 56 | squeeze | | | |
| 57 | squirt | | | |
| 58 | stack | | | |
| 59 | start | | | |
| 60 | stay | | | |
| 61 | stir | | | |
| 62 | stretch | | | |
| 63 | suck | | | |
| 64 | swallow | | | |
| 65 | take | | | |
| 66 | talk | | | |
| 67 | tape | | | |
| 68 | taste | | | |
| 69 | tear | | | |
| 70 | thank | | | |
| 71 | tie | | | |
| 72 | trip | | | |
| 73 | turn | | | |
| 74 | type | | | |
| 75 | unlock | | | |
| 76 | vacuum | | | |
| 77 | wait | | | |
| 78 | wake | | | |
| 79 | watch | | | |
| 80 | wear | | | |

# Verb ~ Set 4

**Objective** _____

| | Target | | | |
|---|---|---|---|---|
| 1 | am | | | |
| 2 | are | | | |
| 3 | be | | | |
| 4 | bet | | | |
| 5 | bless | | | |
| 6 | bother | | | |
| 7 | call | | | |
| 8 | could | | | |
| 9 | die | | | |
| 10 | do | | | |
| 11 | dream | | | |
| 12 | fire | | | |
| 13 | forget | | | |
| 14 | freeze | | | |
| 15 | gobble | | | |
| 16 | got | | | |
| 17 | grab | | | |
| 18 | grow | | | |
| 19 | guess | | | |
| 20 | happen | | | |
| 21 | has | | | |
| 22 | hate | | | |
| 23 | hope | | | |
| 24 | hurry | | | |
| 25 | hush | | | |
| 26 | is | | | |
| 27 | kill | | | |
| 28 | know | | | |
| 29 | let | | | |
| 30 | lift | | | |
| 31 | lose | | | |
| 32 | marry | | | |
| 33 | meet | | | |
| 34 | miss | | | |
| 35 | park | | | |
| 36 | pay | | | |
| 37 | peek | | | |
| 38 | pray | | | |
| 39 | press | | | |
| 40 | raise | | | |

# Verb ~ Set 4

**Objective** _____

| | Target | | | |
|---|---|---|---|---|
| 41 | remember | | | |
| 42 | save | | | |
| 43 | scare | | | |
| 44 | should | | | |
| 45 | slap | | | |
| 46 | sneak | | | |
| 47 | spank | | | |
| 48 | spend | | | |
| 49 | step | | | |
| 50 | stink | | | |
| 51 | tease | | | |
| 52 | tell | | | |
| 53 | think | | | |
| 54 | tip | | | |
| 55 | use | | | |
| 56 | wade | | | |
| 57 | was | | | |
| 58 | waste | | | |
| 59 | were | | | |
| 60 | whip | | | |
| 61 | whisper | | | |
| 62 | will | | | |
| 63 | wind | | | |
| 64 | wink | | | |
| 65 | would | | | |
| 66 | | | | |
| 67 | | | | |
| 68 | | | | |
| 69 | | | | |
| 70 | | | | |
| 71 | | | | |
| 72 | | | | |
| 73 | | | | |
| 74 | | | | |
| 75 | | | | |
| 76 | | | | |
| 77 | | | | |
| 78 | | | | |
| 79 | | | | |
| 80 | | | | |

# Verb ~ Emotion

**Objective** _____

| | Target | | | |
|---|---|---|---|---|
| 1 | angry | | | |
| 2 | confused | | | |
| 3 | embarassed | | | |
| 4 | excited | | | |
| 5 | frustrated | | | |
| 6 | happy | | | |
| 7 | mad | | | |
| 8 | proud | | | |
| 9 | sad | | | |
| 10 | scared | | | |
| 11 | scary | | | |
| 12 | shy | | | |
| 13 | sick | | | |
| 14 | silly | | | |
| 15 | sleepy | | | |
| 16 | surprised | | | |
| 17 | worried | | | |
| 18 | | | | |
| 19 | | | | |
| 20 | | | | |

# Verb ~ Interaction

**Objective** _____

| | Target | | | |
|---|---|---|---|---|
| 1 | arguing | | | |
| 2 | complaining | | | |
| 3 | fighting | | | |
| 4 | hiding | | | |
| 5 | hugging | | | |
| 6 | playing | | | |
| 7 | sharing | | | |
| 8 | talking | | | |
| 9 | teasing | | | |
| 10 | working | | | |
| 11 | | | | |
| 12 | | | | |
| 13 | | | | |
| 14 | | | | |

# Verb ~ Internal Event

**Objective** _____

| Target | | | |
|---|---|---|---|
| 1 bored | | | |
| 2 headache | | | |
| 3 hurt | | | |
| 4 jealous | | | |
| 5 lonely | | | |
| 6 need to go bathroom | | | |
| 7 nervous | | | |
| 8 sad | | | |
| 9 tired | | | |
| 10 toothache | | | |
| 11 | | | |
| 12 | | | |
| 13 | | | |
| 14 | | | |
| 15 | | | |

# Verb ~ Tense

**Objective** _____

| Target | | | |
|---|---|---|---|
| 1 be - was - been | | | |
| 2 begin - began - begun | | | |
| 3 bite - bit - bitten | | | |
| 4 blow - blew - blown | | | |
| 5 break - broke - broken | | | |
| 6 build - built - built | | | |
| 7 buy - bought - bought | | | |
| 8 catch - caught - caught | | | |
| 9 choose - chose - chosen | | | |
| 10 come - came - come | | | |
| 11 cut - cut - cut | | | |
| 12 dig - dug - dug | | | |
| 13 do - did - done | | | |
| 14 draw - drew - drawn | | | |
| 15 eat - ate - eaten | | | |
| 16 fall - fell - fallen | | | |
| 17 feed - fed - fed | | | |
| 18 feel - felt - felt | | | |
| 19 fight - fought - fought | | | |
| 20 fly - flew - flown | | | |

Language Targets to Teach a Child to Communicate

# Verb ~ Tense

**Objective** _____

| Target | | | |
|---|---|---|---|
| 21 freeze - froze - frozen | | | |
| 22 get - got - gotten | | | |
| 23 give - gave - given | | | |
| 24 go - went - gone | | | |
| 25 grow - grew - grown | | | |
| 26 hang - hung - hung | | | |
| 27 have - had - had | | | |
| 28 hide - hid - hidden | | | |
| 29 hold - held - held | | | |
| 30 keep - kept - kept | | | |
| 31 know - knew - known | | | |
| 32 leave - left - left | | | |
| 33 let - let - let | | | |
| 34 lie - lay - lain | | | |
| 35 lose - lost - lost | | | |
| 36 make - made - made | | | |
| 37 pay - paid - paid | | | |
| 38 put - put - put | | | |
| 39 quit - quit - quit | | | |
| 40 ride - rode - ridden | | | |
| 41 run - ran - run | | | |
| 42 say - said - said | | | |
| 43 see - saw - seen | | | |
| 44 sell - sold - sold | | | |
| 45 send - sent - sent | | | |
| 46 shake - shook - shaken | | | |
| 47 shoot - shot - shot | | | |
| 48 shrink - shrank - shrunk | | | |
| 49 sleep - slept - slept | | | |
| 50 slide - slid - slid | | | |
| 51 stand - stood - stood | | | |
| 52 steal - stole - stolen | | | |
| 53 stick - stuck - stuck | | | |
| 54 sweep - swept - swept | | | |
| 55 swim - swam - swum | | | |
| 56 swing - swung - swung | | | |
| 57 take - took - taken | | | |
| 58 tell - told - told | | | |
| 59 wear - wore - worn | | | |
| 60 write - wrote - written | | | |

# Chapter 3 - Receptive Instruction
## Instruction Level 1 ~ Situational Instruction

**Objective** _____

| Target | | | |
|---|---|---|---|
| 1  give me the toy | | | |
| 2  jump | | | |
| 3  point to X | | | |
| 4  put the blocks away | | | |
| 5  raise arm | | | |
| 6  run | | | |
| 7  sit down | | | |
| 8  stand up | | | |
| 9  stomp your feet | | | |
| 10 swing | | | |
| 11 touch your head | | | |
| 12 wave bye bye | | | |
| 13 | | | |
| 14 | | | |

## Instruction Level 2 ~ Object Manipulation

**Objective** _____

| Target | | | |
|---|---|---|---|
| 1  blow bubbles | | | |
| 2  build tower | | | |
| 3  fly airplane | | | |
| 4  hit drum | | | |
| 5  kiss bear | | | |
| 6  play xylophone | | | |
| 7  push wagon | | | |
| 8  put on hat | | | |
| 9  throw ball | | | |
| 10 | | | |
| 11 | | | |
| 12 | | | |
| 13 | | | |
| 14 | | | |
| 15 | | | |
| 16 | | | |
| 17 | | | |
| 18 | | | |
| 19 | | | |
| 20 | | | |

# Instruction Level 3 ~ Fine Motor

**Objective** _____

| Target | | | |
|---|---|---|---|
| 1  blow kiss | | | |
| 2  brush your teeth | | | |
| 3  clap | | | |
| 4  give me 5 | | | |
| 5  put away your cup | | | |
| 6  put on your coat | | | |
| 7  wash your hands | | | |
| 8 | | | |
| 9 | | | |
| 10 | | | |
| 11 | | | |
| 12 | | | |
| 13 | | | |
| 14 | | | |
| 15 | | | |

# Instruction Level 4 ~ Discrimination

**Objective** _____

| Target | | | |
|---|---|---|---|
| 1  Cover the | | | |
| 2  Find the | | | |
| 3  Get the | | | |
| 4  Give me | | | |
| 5  Hand the | | | |
| 6  Name a | | | |
| 7  Open the | | | |
| 8  Pick up | | | |
| 9  Point to | | | |
| 10  Show me | | | |
| 11  Tell me | | | |
| 12  Touch the | | | |
| 13  Which one is | | | |
| 14  Will you | | | |
| 15 | | | |
| 16 | | | |
| 17 | | | |
| 18 | | | |

# Instruction Level 5 ~ Pretend

**Objective** _____

| Target | | | |
|---|---|---|---|
| 1  be a cat | | | |
| 2  be a dog | | | |
| 3  be a lion | | | |
| 4  be a monster | | | |
| 5  brush teeth | | | |
| 6  drink the water | | | |
| 7  drive the car | | | |
| 8  eat a cookie | | | |
| 9  ride the horse | | | |
| 10  sleep | | | |
| 11  snore | | | |
| 12  talk on telephone | | | |
| 13 | | | |
| 14 | | | |
| 15 | | | |
| 16 | | | |
| 17 | | | |

# Instruction Level 6 ~ Gross Motor Movement

**Objective** _____

| Target | | | |
|---|---|---|---|
| 1  close the door | | | |
| 2  go sit in the corner | | | |
| 3  hop on one foot | | | |
| 4  put this in the box | | | |
| 5  throw this away | | | |
| 6  turn around | | | |
| 7  turn on the light | | | |
| 8 | | | |
| 9 | | | |
| 10 | | | |
| 11 | | | |
| 12 | | | |
| 13 | | | |
| 14 | | | |
| 15 | | | |
| 16 | | | |
| 17 | | | |

# Instruction Level 7 ~ Advanced Object

**Objective** _____

| Target | | | |
|---|---|---|---|
| 1 Give me A, B | | | |
| 2 Give me A, B, and C | | | |
| 3 Give me A and B and clap your hands | | | |
| 4 Put the X under the Y | | | |
| 5 Put the X on the Y and the A under the B | | | |
| 6 Put the X on the W and stomp your feet | | | |
| 7 Hug Pooh and put Owl in the bed. | | | |
| 8 Feed the fries to Barney and kiss Woody | | | |
| 9 Put the book away and touch your head. | | | |
| 10 | | | |
| 11 | | | |
| 12 | | | |
| 13 | | | |
| 14 | | | |
| 15 | | | |
| 16 | | | |
| 17 | | | |

# Instruction Level 8 ~ Gross Motor Movement

**Objective** _____

| Target | | | |
|---|---|---|---|
| 1 Give this to named person | | | |
| 2 Go see named person | | | |
| 3 Go to named person and get the book. | | | |
| 4 Go to named person and shake her hand. | | | |
| 5 Go to X and get A and B | | | |
| 6 Go to X and get Y and go to Z and get W | | | |
| 7 | | | |
| 8 | | | |
| 9 | | | |
| 10 | | | |
| 11 | | | |
| 12 | | | |
| 13 | | | |
| 14 | | | |
| 15 | | | |
| 16 | | | |
| 17 | | | |

# Chapter 4 - Word Association
## Animal Sound

**Objective** _____

| | Target | | | |
|---|---|---|---|---|
| 1 | bee says buzz | | | |
| 2 | bird says tweet tweet | | | |
| 3 | cat says meow | | | |
| 4 | chicken says cheep cheep | | | |
| 5 | cow says moo | | | |
| 6 | crow says caw | | | |
| 7 | dog says woof woof | | | |
| 8 | donkey say hee haw | | | |
| 9 | duck says quack | | | |
| 10 | frog says ribbit | | | |
| 11 | horse says neigh | | | |
| 12 | lion says roar | | | |
| 13 | mouse says eek | | | |
| 14 | owl says who who | | | |
| 15 | pig says oink | | | |
| 16 | rooster says cock-a-doodle-doo | | | |
| 17 | sheep says baa baa | | | |
| 18 | snake says hiss | | | |
| 19 | turkey says gobble | | | |
| 20 | | | | |
| 21 | | | | |
| 22 | | | | |
| 23 | | | | |
| 24 | | | | |
| 25 | | | | |
| 26 | | | | |
| 27 | | | | |
| 28 | | | | |
| 29 | | | | |
| 30 | | | | |
| 31 | | | | |
| 32 | | | | |
| 33 | | | | |
| 34 | | | | |
| 35 | | | | |
| 36 | | | | |
| 37 | | | | |
| 38 | | | | |
| 39 | | | | |

# Fill In The Blank

**Objective** _____

| Target | | | |
|---|---|---|---|
| 1  blow your ____nose | | | |
| 2  brush your _____teeth | | | |
| 3  clap your _____ hands | | | |
| 4  clean up the _____mess | | | |
| 5  close your _____eyes | | | |
| 6  don't fall _____down | | | |
| 7  drink your _____juice | | | |
| 8  drive the _____car | | | |
| 9  dry off with the ____towel | | | |
| 10  feed the _____dog | | | |
| 11  finish your _____work | | | |
| 12  fly a _____kite | | | |
| 13  gobble you ____up | | | |
| 14  good ____bye | | | |
| 15  hang up your ____coat | | | |
| 16  I'm going to get _____you | | | |
| 17  knock knock _____who's there | | | |
| 18  lay down in ____bed | | | |
| 19  listen to _____music | | | |
| 20  one, two, _____three | | | |
| 21  open the _____door | | | |
| 22  peek – a – ____boo | | | |
| 23  pet the _____cat | | | |
| 24  pull up your ____pants | | | |
| 25  push the _____button | | | |
| 26  raise your _____hand | | | |
| 27  ready – set – ____go | | | |
| 28  run for your _____life | | | |
| 29  sing a _____song | | | |
| 30  skip to my _____lou | | | |
| 31  stomp your _____feet | | | |
| 32  take off your _____shoes | | | |
| 33  this little piggy | | | |
| 34  throw the _____ball | | | |
| 35  tickle your _____toes | | | |
| 36  tie my _____shoes | | | |
| 37  time to go to _____bed | | | |
| 38  turn on the ____TV | | | |
| 39  wash your ____hands | | | |
| 40  wipe your _____nose | | | |

# Noun and Noun

**Objective** _____

| Target | | | |
|---|---|---|---|
| 1 bacon and eggs | | | |
| 2 basketball and hoop | | | |
| 3 bat and ball | | | |
| 4 boy and girl | | | |
| 5 bread and butter | | | |
| 6 brush and paint | | | |
| 7 candles and birthday cake | | | |
| 8 cheese and crackers | | | |
| 9 comb and brush | | | |
| 10 fork and knife | | | |
| 11 glove and hand | | | |
| 12 hammer and nail | | | |
| 13 hat and head | | | |
| 14 king and queen | | | |
| 15 knife and fork | | | |
| 16 milk and cookies | | | |
| 17 moon and stars | | | |
| 18 mother and father | | | |
| 19 peanut butter and jelly | | | |
| 20 pencil and paper | | | |
| 21 pillow and bed | | | |
| 22 ring and finger | | | |
| 23 salt and pepper | | | |
| 24 shovel and pail | | | |
| 25 socks and shoes | | | |
| 26 spider and web | | | |
| 27 table and chair | | | |
| 28 toothbrush and toothpaste | | | |
| 29 train and track | | | |
| 30 VCR and TV | | | |
| 31 | | | |
| 32 | | | |
| 33 | | | |
| 34 | | | |
| 35 | | | |
| 36 | | | |
| 37 | | | |
| 38 | | | |
| 39 | | | |
| 40 | | | |

# Object Sound

**Objective** _____

| Target | | | |
|---|---|---|---|
| 1 baby goes wa wa | | | |
| 2 bubble goes pop | | | |
| 3 car goes beep beep | | | |
| 4 clock goes tick tock | | | |
| 5 doorbell goes ding dong | | | |
| 6 drum goes boom boom | | | |
| 7 hands go clap | | | |
| 8 horn goes honk | | | |
| 9 piano goes de da la | | | |
| 10 rain goes splish splash | | | |
| 11 siren goes whoo whoo | | | |
| 12 telephone goes ring ring | | | |
| 13 train goes choo choo | | | |
| 14 wipers goes swish swish | | | |
| 15 | | | |
| 16 | | | |
| 17 | | | |
| 18 | | | |
| 19 | | | |
| 20 | | | |
| 21 | | | |
| 22 | | | |
| 23 | | | |
| 24 | | | |
| 25 | | | |
| 26 | | | |
| 27 | | | |
| 28 | | | |
| 29 | | | |
| 30 | | | |
| 31 | | | |
| 32 | | | |
| 33 | | | |
| 34 | | | |
| 35 | | | |
| 36 | | | |
| 37 | | | |
| 38 | | | |
| 39 | | | |
| 40 | | | |

# Opposite

**Objective** _____

| Target | | | |
|---|---|---|---|
| 1 alive - dead | | | |
| 2 all - none | | | |
| 3 alone - together | | | |
| 4 asleep - awake | | | |
| 5 away - toward | | | |
| 6 before - after | | | |
| 7 beginning - end | | | |
| 8 big - little | | | |
| 9 black - white | | | |
| 10 boy - girl | | | |
| 11 broken - fixed | | | |
| 12 clean - dirty | | | |
| 13 come - go | | | |
| 14 day - night | | | |
| 15 empty - full | | | |
| 16 fat - skinny | | | |
| 17 first - last | | | |
| 18 flat - bumpy | | | |
| 19 friend - enemy | | | |
| 20 front - back | | | |
| 21 get - give | | | |
| 22 good - bad | | | |
| 23 hairy - bald | | | |
| 24 happy - sad | | | |
| 25 he - she | | | |
| 26 heavy - light | | | |
| 27 help - hurt | | | |
| 28 hot - cold | | | |
| 29 hungry - stuffed | | | |
| 30 in - out | | | |
| 31 large - tiny | | | |
| 32 late - early | | | |
| 33 laugh - cry | | | |
| 34 lazy - working | | | |
| 35 light - dark | | | |
| 36 loose - tight | | | |
| 37 make - destroy | | | |
| 38 man - woman | | | |
| 39 many - few | | | |
| 40 messy - neat | | | |

# Opposite

**Objective** _____

| Target | | | |
|---|---|---|---|
| 41 move – stay | | | |
| 42 mushy – firm | | | |
| 43 never – always | | | |
| 44 old - new | | | |
| 45 on - off | | | |
| 46 one - several | | | |
| 47 open - closed | | | |
| 48 other - same | | | |
| 49 over - under | | | |
| 50 pretty - ugly | | | |
| 51 push - pull | | | |
| 52 question - answer | | | |
| 53 right - left | | | |
| 54 rough - smooth | | | |
| 55 salty - sweet | | | |
| 56 short - long | | | |
| 57 sit - stand | | | |
| 58 slow - fast | | | |
| 59 smart - stupid | | | |
| 60 soft - hard | | | |
| 61 stop - go | | | |
| 62 thin - thick | | | |
| 63 to - from | | | |
| 64 top - bottom | | | |
| 65 up - down | | | |
| 66 warm - cool | | | |
| 67 wet - dry | | | |
| 68 wide - narrow | | | |
| 69 work - play | | | |
| 70 yes - no | | | |
| 71 young - old | | | |
| 72 yummy - yucky | | | |
| 73 | | | |
| 74 | | | |
| 75 | | | |
| 76 | | | |
| 77 | | | |
| 78 | | | |
| 79 | | | |
| 80 | | | |

# Song or Poem

**Objective** _____

| Target | | | |
|---|---|---|---|
| 1 | A Tisket a Tasket | | |
| 2 | Ba Ba Black Sheep | | |
| 3 | Bingo | | |
| 4 | Down by the Station | | |
| 5 | Frere Jacques | | |
| 6 | Head Shoulders Knees and Toes | | |
| 7 | Hey Diddle Diddle | | |
| 8 | Hickory Dickory Dock | | |
| 9 | Hokey Pokey | | |
| 10 | How Much Is That Doggie? | | |
| 11 | If Your Happy and You Know It | | |
| 12 | Its Raining Its Pouring | | |
| 13 | Itsy Bitsy Spider | | |
| 14 | I've been working on the railroad | | |
| 15 | John Jacob Jingle Heimer Schmidt | | |
| 16 | Little Bo Peep | | |
| 17 | Little Boy Blue | | |
| 18 | Little Miss Muffet | | |
| 19 | London Bridges | | |
| 20 | Mary Had a Little Lamb | | |
| 21 | Michael Row Your Boat Ashore | | |
| 22 | Oh Dear What Can the Matter Be? | | |
| 23 | Oh Susanna | | |
| 24 | Old MacDonald Had a Farm | | |
| 25 | Pop Goes the Weasel | | |
| 26 | Row Row Row Your Boat | | |
| 27 | She'll be Coming Around the Mountain | | |
| 28 | The Ants Go Marching | | |
| 29 | The Bear Went Over the Mountain. | | |
| 30 | The More We Get Together | | |
| 31 | The Muffin Man | | |
| 32 | The Wheels on the Bus | | |
| 33 | This Little Light of Mine | | |
| 34 | This Little Piggy Went To Market | | |
| 35 | This Old Man | | |
| 36 | Three Blind Mice | | |
| 37 | Twinkle Twinkle | | |
| 38 | | | |
| 39 | | | |
| 40 | | | |

# Synonym

**Objective** _____

| Target | | | |
|---|---|---|---|
| 1 after – behind | | | |
| 2 all – every | | | |
| 3 begin – start | | | |
| 4 big – large – gigantic | | | |
| 5 boy – male | | | |
| 6 buddy – friend | | | |
| 7 call – shout | | | |
| 8 car – automobile | | | |
| 9 close – shut | | | |
| 10 easy – simple | | | |
| 11 end – finish | | | |
| 12 girl – female | | | |
| 13 give – hand | | | |
| 14 go – leave | | | |
| 15 keep – hold | | | |
| 16 kids – children | | | |
| 17 like – enjoy | | | |
| 18 listen – hear | | | |
| 19 look – see | | | |
| 20 loud – noisy | | | |
| 21 make – build | | | |
| 22 mix – stir | | | |
| 23 night – evening | | | |
| 24 one – single | | | |
| 25 over - above | | | |
| 26 picture – photo | | | |
| 27 right – correct | | | |
| 28 small – little – tiny | | | |
| 29 take – grab | | | |
| 30 talk – speak | | | |
| 31 | | | |
| 32 | | | |
| 33 | | | |
| 34 | | | |
| 35 | | | |
| 36 | | | |
| 37 | | | |
| 38 | | | |
| 39 | | | |
| 40 | | | |

# Chapter 5 - Communication
## Communication ~ Affirmative

**Objective** _____

| | Target | | | |
|---|---|---|---|---|
| 1 | alright | | | |
| 2 | okay | | | |
| 3 | right | | | |
| 4 | sure | | | |
| 5 | yes | | | |
| 6 | | | | |
| 7 | | | | |

## Communication ~ Functional

**Objective** _____

| | Target | | | |
|---|---|---|---|---|
| 1 | Bless you | | | |
| 2 | Can I? | | | |
| 3 | Come in. | | | |
| 4 | Come on | | | |
| 5 | Don't do that. | | | |
| 6 | Excuse me. | | | |
| 7 | Get me. | | | |
| 8 | Give me that. | | | |
| 9 | Go away. | | | |
| 10 | Good job | | | |
| 11 | Help me. | | | |
| 12 | Here I am. | | | |
| 13 | I am sick. | | | |
| 14 | I am sorry. | | | |
| 15 | I am tired. | | | |
| 16 | I can't wait. | | | |
| 17 | I did it | | | |
| 18 | I don't care. | | | |
| 19 | I don't know. | | | |
| 20 | I don't understand | | | |
| 21 | I don't want to | | | |
| 22 | I'm all done. | | | |
| 23 | I'm ready. | | | |
| 24 | Is that ok? | | | |
| 25 | It's for you | | | |

# Communication ~ Functional

**Objective** _____

| Target | | | |
|---|---|---|---|
| 26 It's my turn. | | | |
| 27 Leave me alone. | | | |
| 28 Let me see. | | | |
| 29 Let's go | | | |
| 30 Let's play | | | |
| 31 Look at me. | | | |
| 32 Look at that. | | | |
| 33 Look out. | | | |
| 34 Move please. | | | |
| 35 My turn. | | | |
| 36 No way | | | |
| 37 Over there | | | |
| 38 Peekaboo | | | |
| 39 Please | | | |
| 40 Quiet | | | |
| 41 Ready | | | |
| 42 Ready set go | | | |
| 43 Stop it | | | |
| 44 Thank you | | | |
| 45 Thanks | | | |
| 46 That one | | | |
| 47 That's mine | | | |
| 48 This one. | | | |
| 49 Tickle me. | | | |
| 50 Too bad | | | |
| 51 Wanna play | | | |
| 52 Watch out. | | | |
| 53 | | | |
| 54 | | | |

# Communication ~ Greeting

**Objective** _____

| Target | | | |
|---|---|---|---|
| 1 Bye | | | |
| 2 Hello | | | |
| 3 Hey | | | |
| 4 Hi | | | |
| 5 See ya later | | | |

# Communication ~ Interjection

**Objective** _____

| Target | | | |
|---|---|---|---|
| 1 cool | | | |
| 2 darn | | | |
| 3 hooray | | | |
| 4 oh | | | |
| 5 oh no | | | |
| 6 ouch | | | |
| 7 owee | | | |
| 8 phooey | | | |
| 9 shoot | | | |
| 10 surprise | | | |
| 11 tah dah | | | |
| 12 uh oh | | | |
| 13 whoops | | | |
| 14 wow | | | |
| 15 yuk | | | |
| 16 yummy | | | |
| 17 | | | |
| 18 | | | |
| 19 | | | |
| 20 | | | |

# Communication ~ Negative

**Objective** _____

| Target | | | |
|---|---|---|---|
| 1 can't | | | |
| 2 couldn't | | | |
| 3 don't | | | |
| 4 no | | | |
| 5 no thanks | | | |
| 6 not | | | |
| 7 shouldn't | | | |
| 8 won't | | | |
| 9 wouldn't | | | |
| 10 | | | |
| 11 | | | |
| 12 | | | |
| 13 | | | |
| 14 | | | |

# Chapter 6 - Advanced Single Word
## Adjective

**Objective** _____

| | Target | | | |
|---|---|---|---|---|
| 1 | afraid | | | |
| 2 | alone | | | |
| 3 | angry | | | |
| 4 | apart | | | |
| 5 | asleep | | | |
| 6 | awake | | | |
| 7 | backward | | | |
| 8 | bad | | | |
| 9 | beautiful | | | |
| 10 | best | | | |
| 11 | better | | | |
| 12 | big | | | |
| 13 | bored | | | |
| 14 | bright | | | |
| 15 | broken | | | |
| 16 | busy | | | |
| 17 | careful | | | |
| 18 | chilly | | | |
| 19 | clean | | | |
| 20 | closed | | | |
| 21 | clumsy | | | |
| 22 | cold | | | |
| 23 | cool | | | |
| 24 | crazy | | | |
| 25 | cute | | | |
| 26 | dangerous | | | |
| 27 | dark | | | |
| 28 | dead | | | |
| 29 | different | | | |
| 30 | difficult | | | |
| 31 | dirty | | | |
| 32 | dizzy | | | |
| 33 | dry | | | |
| 34 | early | | | |
| 35 | easy | | | |
| 36 | empty | | | |
| 37 | even | | | |
| 38 | fat | | | |
| 39 | favorite | | | |
| 40 | fine | | | |

# Adjective

**Objective** _____

| | Target | | | |
|---|---|---|---|---|
| 41 | fixed | | | |
| 42 | flat | | | |
| 43 | fresh | | | |
| 44 | friendly | | | |
| 45 | front | | | |
| 46 | frozen | | | |
| 47 | full | | | |
| 48 | funny | | | |
| 49 | furry | | | |
| 50 | fuzzy | | | |
| 51 | gentle | | | |
| 52 | gigantic | | | |
| 53 | gone | | | |
| 54 | good | | | |
| 55 | gorgeous | | | |
| 56 | great | | | |
| 57 | grumpy | | | |
| 58 | handsome | | | |
| 59 | happy | | | |
| 60 | hard | | | |
| 61 | healthy | | | |
| 62 | heavy | | | |
| 63 | high | | | |
| 64 | horrible | | | |
| 65 | hot | | | |
| 66 | hungry | | | |
| 67 | hurt | | | |
| 68 | itchy | | | |
| 69 | jolly | | | |
| 70 | just | | | |
| 71 | kind | | | |
| 72 | large | | | |
| 73 | last | | | |
| 74 | late | | | |
| 75 | light | | | |
| 76 | little | | | |
| 77 | long | | | |
| 78 | low | | | |
| 79 | mad | | | |
| 80 | mean | | | |

# Adjective

**Objective** _____

| | Target | | | |
|---|---|---|---|---|
| 81 | medium | | | |
| 82 | melted | | | |
| 83 | messy | | | |
| 84 | middle | | | |
| 85 | mighty | | | |
| 86 | mushy | | | |
| 87 | naked | | | |
| 88 | narrow | | | |
| 89 | nasty | | | |
| 90 | naughty | | | |
| 91 | neat | | | |
| 92 | new | | | |
| 93 | nice | | | |
| 94 | noisy | | | |
| 95 | odd | | | |
| 96 | old | | | |
| 97 | only | | | |
| 98 | open | | | |
| 99 | poor | | | |
| 100 | pretty | | | |
| 101 | quick | | | |
| 102 | quiet | | | |
| 103 | rainy | | | |
| 104 | rare | | | |
| 105 | ratty | | | |
| 106 | right | | | |
| 107 | rough | | | |
| 108 | round | | | |
| 109 | salty | | | |
| 110 | same | | | |
| 111 | scary | | | |
| 112 | scratchy | | | |
| 113 | scrawny | | | |
| 114 | sharp | | | |
| 115 | short | | | |
| 116 | sick | | | |
| 117 | silly | | | |
| 118 | skinny | | | |
| 119 | small | | | |
| 120 | smooth | | | |

# Adjective

**Objective** _____

| | Target | | | |
|---|---|---|---|---|
| 121 | soft | | | |
| 122 | sore | | | |
| 123 | sorry | | | |
| 124 | sour | | | |
| 125 | spotty | | | |
| 126 | sticky | | | |
| 127 | still | | | |
| 128 | stinky | | | |
| 129 | straight | | | |
| 130 | strange | | | |
| 131 | striped | | | |
| 132 | strong | | | |
| 133 | stuck | | | |
| 134 | stupid | | | |
| 135 | super | | | |
| 136 | sweet | | | |
| 137 | tall | | | |
| 138 | tame | | | |
| 139 | tart | | | |
| 140 | tender | | | |
| 141 | thin | | | |
| 142 | thirsty | | | |
| 143 | tight | | | |
| 144 | tiny | | | |
| 145 | together | | | |
| 146 | tough | | | |
| 147 | tricky | | | |
| 148 | ugly | | | |
| 149 | upside down | | | |
| 150 | very | | | |
| 151 | warm | | | |
| 152 | watery | | | |
| 153 | well | | | |
| 154 | wet | | | |
| 155 | wide | | | |
| 156 | wonderful | | | |
| 157 | wrong | | | |
| 158 | yet | | | |
| 159 | young | | | |
| 160 | yucky | | | |
| 161 | yummy | | | |

# Adverb

**Objective** _____

| Target | | | |
|---|---|---|---|
| 1 almost | | | |
| 2 badly | | | |
| 3 carefully | | | |
| 4 easily | | | |
| 5 fast | | | |
| 6 loudly | | | |
| 7 oclock | | | |
| 8 quickly | | | |
| 9 quietly | | | |
| 10 slowly | | | |
| 11 too | | | |
| 12 | | | |
| 13 | | | |
| 14 | | | |
| 15 | | | |
| 16 | | | |
| 17 | | | |
| 18 | | | |
| 19 | | | |
| 20 | | | |
| 21 | | | |
| 22 | | | |
| 23 | | | |
| 24 | | | |
| 25 | | | |

# Article

**Objective** _____

| Target | | | |
|---|---|---|---|
| 1 a | | | |
| 2 an | | | |
| 3 the | | | |
| 4 | | | |
| 5 | | | |

# Comparative

**Objective** _____

| | Target | | | |
|---|---|---|---|---|
| 1 | bigger | | | |
| 2 | colder | | | |
| 3 | faster | | | |
| 4 | hotter | | | |
| 5 | longer | | | |
| 6 | older | | | |
| 7 | shorter | | | |
| 8 | slower | | | |
| 9 | smaller | | | |
| 10 | younger | | | |
| 11 | | | | |
| 12 | | | | |
| 13 | | | | |
| 14 | | | | |
| 15 | | | | |

# Conjunction

**Objective** _____

| | Target | | | |
|---|---|---|---|---|
| 1 | after | | | |
| 2 | and | | | |
| 3 | as | | | |
| 4 | because | | | |
| 5 | but | | | |
| 6 | either | | | |
| 7 | for | | | |
| 8 | if | | | |
| 9 | neither | | | |
| 10 | or | | | |
| 11 | since | | | |
| 12 | so | | | |
| 13 | still | | | |
| 14 | than | | | |
| 15 | then | | | |
| 16 | though | | | |
| 17 | till | | | |
| 18 | unless | | | |
| 19 | until | | | |
| 20 | while | | | |

# Preposition

**Objective** _____

| | Target | | | |
|---|---|---|---|---|
| 1 | about | | | |
| 2 | above | | | |
| 3 | across | | | |
| 4 | along | | | |
| 5 | around | | | |
| 6 | at | | | |
| 7 | away | | | |
| 8 | back | | | |
| 9 | beside | | | |
| 10 | between | | | |
| 11 | bottom | | | |
| 12 | by | | | |
| 13 | down | | | |
| 14 | for | | | |
| 15 | forth | | | |
| 16 | from | | | |
| 17 | here | | | |
| 18 | in | | | |
| 19 | in back of | | | |
| 20 | in front of | | | |
| 21 | into | | | |
| 22 | near | | | |
| 23 | next to | | | |
| 24 | of | | | |
| 25 | off | | | |
| 26 | on | | | |
| 27 | onto | | | |
| 28 | out | | | |
| 29 | over | | | |
| 30 | there | | | |
| 31 | through | | | |
| 32 | to | | | |
| 33 | top | | | |
| 34 | under | | | |
| 35 | up | | | |
| 36 | with | | | |
| 37 | without | | | |
| 38 | | | | |
| 39 | | | | |
| 40 | | | | |

# Pronoun ~ Demonstrative

**Objective** _____

| Target | | | |
|---|---|---|---|
| 1 that | | | |
| 2 these | | | |
| 3 this | | | |
| 4 those | | | |

# Pronoun ~ Indefinite

**Objective** _____

| Target | | | |
|---|---|---|---|
| 1 anybody | | | |
| 2 anyone | | | |
| 3 anything | | | |
| 4 everybody | | | |
| 5 everyone | | | |
| 6 everything | | | |
| 7 no one | | | |
| 8 nobody | | | |
| 9 nothing | | | |
| 10 somebody | | | |
| 11 someone | | | |
| 12 something | | | |

# Pronoun ~ Objective

**Objective** _____

| Target | | | |
|---|---|---|---|
| 1 he | | | |
| 2 her | | | |
| 3 him | | | |
| 4 I | | | |
| 5 it | | | |
| 6 me | | | |
| 7 she | | | |
| 8 them | | | |
| 9 they | | | |
| 10 us | | | |
| 11 we | | | |
| 12 you | | | |

Language Targets to Teach a Child to Communicate

# Pronoun ~ Personal

**Objective** _____

| Target | | | |
|---|---|---|---|
| 1  hers | | | |
| 2  his | | | |
| 3  mine | | | |
| 4  my | | | |
| 5  our | | | |
| 6  ours | | | |
| 7  their | | | |
| 8  theirs | | | |
| 9  your | | | |
| 10 yours | | | |
| 11 | | | |
| 12 | | | |
| 13 | | | |
| 14 | | | |
| 15 | | | |

# Pronoun ~ Possessive

**Objective** _____

| Target | | | |
|---|---|---|---|
| 1  herself | | | |
| 2  himself | | | |
| 3  itself | | | |
| 4  myself | | | |
| 5  ourselves | | | |
| 6  themselves | | | |
| 7  yourself | | | |
| 8  yourselves | | | |
| 9 | | | |
| 10 | | | |
| 11 | | | |
| 12 | | | |
| 13 | | | |
| 14 | | | |
| 15 | | | |

# Quantifier

**Objective** _____

| | Target | | | |
|---|---|---|---|---|
| 1 | a lot of | | | |
| 2 | all | | | |
| 3 | also | | | |
| 4 | another | | | |
| 5 | any | | | |
| 6 | bit | | | |
| 7 | bite | | | |
| 8 | both | | | |
| 9 | bunch | | | |
| 10 | couple | | | |
| 11 | each | | | |
| 12 | else | | | |
| 13 | enough | | | |
| 14 | every | | | |
| 15 | few | | | |
| 16 | half | | | |
| 17 | least | | | |
| 18 | less | | | |
| 19 | lots of | | | |
| 20 | many | | | |
| 21 | more | | | |
| 22 | most | | | |
| 23 | much | | | |
| 24 | none | | | |
| 25 | other | | | |
| 26 | pair | | | |
| 27 | part | | | |
| 28 | piece | | | |
| 29 | plenty of | | | |
| 30 | rest | | | |
| 31 | several | | | |
| 32 | some | | | |
| 33 | whole | | | |
| 34 | | | | |
| 35 | | | | |
| 36 | | | | |
| 37 | | | | |
| 38 | | | | |
| 39 | | | | |
| 40 | | | | |

# Time

**Objective** _____

| | Target | | | |
|---|---|---|---|---|
| 1 | 1:00 | | | |
| 2 | 10:00 | | | |
| 3 | 11:00 | | | |
| 4 | 12:00 | | | |
| 5 | 2:00 | | | |
| 6 | 3:00 | | | |
| 7 | 4:00 | | | |
| 8 | 5:00 | | | |
| 9 | 6:00 | | | |
| 10 | 7:00 | | | |
| 11 | 8:00 | | | |
| 12 | 9:00 | | | |
| 13 | after | | | |
| 14 | afternoon | | | |
| 15 | again | | | |
| 16 | already | | | |
| 17 | always | | | |
| 18 | before | | | |
| 19 | day | | | |
| 20 | evening | | | |
| 21 | hour | | | |
| 22 | later | | | |
| 23 | midnight | | | |
| 24 | minute | | | |
| 25 | morning | | | |
| 26 | never | | | |
| 27 | night | | | |
| 28 | noon | | | |
| 29 | now | | | |
| 30 | once | | | |
| 31 | sometime | | | |
| 32 | today | | | |
| 33 | tomorrow | | | |
| 34 | tonight | | | |
| 35 | week | | | |
| 36 | year | | | |
| 37 | yesterday | | | |
| 38 | | | | |
| 39 | | | | |
| 40 | | | | |

# Chapter 7 - Word Relationship
# Category

**Objective** _____

| | Target | | | |
|---|---|---|---|---|
| 1 | aircraft | | | |
| 2 | animals | | | |
| 3 | authors | | | |
| 4 | bathroom things | | | |
| 5 | beach things | | | |
| 6 | bedroom things | | | |
| 7 | birds | | | |
| 8 | bodies of water | | | |
| 9 | body parts | | | |
| 10 | books | | | |
| 11 | buildings | | | |
| 12 | candy | | | |
| 13 | clothes | | | |
| 14 | cold things | | | |
| 15 | colors | | | |
| 16 | community helpers | | | |
| 17 | continents | | | |
| 18 | days | | | |
| 19 | deserts | | | |
| 20 | dishes | | | |
| 21 | drinks | | | |
| 22 | face | | | |
| 23 | fairy tale | | | |
| 24 | family | | | |
| 25 | farm things | | | |
| 26 | fly things | | | |
| 27 | food | | | |
| 28 | food wear | | | |
| 29 | fruit | | | |
| 30 | furniture | | | |
| 31 | games | | | |
| 32 | holidays | | | |
| 33 | hot things | | | |
| 34 | insects | | | |
| 35 | instruments | | | |
| 36 | jewelry | | | |
| 37 | kitchen | | | |
| 38 | land form | | | |
| 39 | letters | | | |
| 40 | meat | | | |

# Category

**Objective** _____

| | Target | | | |
|---|---|---|---|---|
| 41 | money | | | |
| 42 | nature | | | |
| 43 | numbers | | | |
| 44 | outside | | | |
| 45 | people | | | |
| 46 | plants | | | |
| 47 | playground | | | |
| 48 | rooms | | | |
| 49 | school things | | | |
| 50 | seasons | | | |
| 51 | seven dwarfs | | | |
| 52 | shapes | | | |
| 53 | sick things | | | |
| 54 | signs | | | |
| 55 | silverware | | | |
| 56 | sky things | | | |
| 57 | snacks | | | |
| 58 | songs | | | |
| 59 | space | | | |
| 60 | sports | | | |
| 61 | summer time | | | |
| 62 | things that grow | | | |
| 63 | tools | | | |
| 64 | toys | | | |
| 65 | vegetables | | | |
| 66 | vehicles | | | |
| 67 | videos | | | |
| 68 | weather | | | |
| 69 | winter time | | | |
| 70 | | | | |
| 71 | | | | |
| 72 | | | | |
| 73 | | | | |
| 74 | | | | |
| 75 | | | | |
| 76 | | | | |
| 77 | | | | |
| 78 | | | | |
| 79 | | | | |
| 80 | | | | |

# Category + 1 Adjective

**Objective** _____

| Target | | | |
|---|---|---|---|
| 1  animals – farm | | | |
| 2  animals – forest | | | |
| 3  animals – insects | | | |
| 4  animals – ocean | | | |
| 5  animals – pets | | | |
| 6  animals – zoo | | | |
| 7  drink – cold | | | |
| 8  drink – hot | | | |
| 9  drink – sweet | | | |
| 10  food – breakfast | | | |
| 11  food – cold | | | |
| 12  food – dinner | | | |
| 13  food – hot | | | |
| 14  food – lunch | | | |
| 15  food – salty | | | |
| 16  vehicle – 2 wheels | | | |
| 17  vehicle – 4 wheels | | | |
| 18 | | | |
| 19 | | | |
| 20 | | | |
| 21 | | | |
| 22 | | | |
| 23 | | | |
| 24 | | | |

# Category + 2 Adjectives

**Objective** _____

| Target | | | |
|---|---|---|---|
| 1  big farm animal | | | |
| 2  big forest animal | | | |
| 3  crunchy salty food | | | |
| 4  small farm animal | | | |
| 5  soft sweet food | | | |
| 6 | | | |
| 7 | | | |
| 8 | | | |
| 9 | | | |
| 10 | | | |

Language Targets to Teach a Child to Communicate

# Category ~ Is A Category

**Objective** _____

| Target | | | |
|---|---|---|---|
| 1 blue – sky | | | |
| 2 bright – sun | | | |
| 3 brown – horse | | | |
| 4 cold – ice | | | |
| 5 fast – motorcycle | | | |
| 6 furry – cat | | | |
| 7 gray – elephant | | | |
| 8 green – grass | | | |
| 9 hot – fire | | | |
| 10 long – snake | | | |
| 11 orange – carrot | | | |
| 12 rectangle – dollar | | | |
| 13 red – apple | | | |
| 14 round – ball | | | |
| 15 salty – chips | | | |
| 16 sharp – knife | | | |
| 17 slow – turtle | | | |
| 18 small – pea | | | |
| 19 sticky – glue | | | |
| 20 stinky – poop | | | |
| 21 sweet – candy | | | |
| 22 tall – giraffe | | | |
| 23 white – snow | | | |
| 24 yellow – banana | | | |

# Category ~ Type of

**Objective** _____

| Target | | | |
|---|---|---|---|
| 1 A is a letter | | | |
| 2 A is in the alphabet | | | |
| 3 airplane is something in the sky | | | |
| 4 airplane is a vehicle | | | |
| 5 ambulance is a vehicle | | | |
| 6 ant is a bug | | | |
| 7 ant is an insect | | | |
| 8 baby is a person | | | |
| 9 bacon is hot | | | |
| 10 bacon is meat | | | |

# Category ~ Type of

**Objective** _____

| Target | | | |
|---|---|---|---|
| 11  ball is something round | | | |
| 12  ball is a toy | | | |
| 13  banana is a food | | | |
| 14  banana is a fruit | | | |
| 15  baseball is a sport | | | |
| 16  bathing suit is clothing | | | |
| 17  beach is a place | | | |
| 18  bed is furniture | | | |
| 19  bike is a vehicle | | | |
| 20  blue is a color | | | |
| 21  boy is a child | | | |
| 22  boy is a person | | | |
| 23  cake is a desert | | | |
| 24  car is a toy | | | |
| 25  car is a vehicle | | | |
| 26  carrots are a vegetable | | | |
| 27  cat is an animal | | | |
| 28  chips are a salty food | | | |
| 29  chips are a snack | | | |
| 30  Christmas is a holiday | | | |
| 31  circle is a shape | | | |
| 32  coat is clothing | | | |
| 33  cow is a farm animal | | | |
| 34  dad is a man | | | |
| 35  dad is a parent | | | |
| 36  dad is a person | | | |
| 37  dad is an adult | | | |
| 38  dog is a pet | | | |
| 39  dog is an animal | | | |
| 40  Dr. Seuss is an author | | | |
| 41  drum is an instrument | | | |
| 42  egg is a breakfast food | | | |
| 43  elephant is a zoo animal | | | |
| 44  firefighter is a community helper | | | |
| 45  firefighter is a person | | | |
| 46  flower is a plant | | | |
| 47  hammer is a tool | | | |
| 48  hammer is a toy | | | |
| 49  horse is a farm animal | | | |
| 50  horse is a mammal | | | |

# Category ~ Type of

**Objective** _____

| | Target | | | |
|---|---|---|---|---|
| 51 | juice is a drink | | | |
| 52 | microwave is an appliance | | | |
| 53 | milk is a drink | | | |
| 54 | milk is something in the refrigerator | | | |
| 55 | mom is a parent | | | |
| 56 | mom is a woman | | | |
| 57 | nose is a body part | | | |
| 58 | nose is on your face | | | |
| 59 | quarter is a coin | | | |
| 60 | quarter is money | | | |
| 61 | shirt is clothing | | | |
| 62 | shoes are footwear | | | |
| 63 | store is a building | | | |
| 64 | table is furniture | | | |
| 65 | | | | |
| 66 | | | | |
| 67 | | | | |
| 68 | | | | |
| 69 | | | | |
| 70 | | | | |
| 71 | | | | |
| 72 | | | | |
| 73 | | | | |
| 74 | | | | |
| 75 | | | | |
| 76 | | | | |
| 77 | | | | |
| 78 | | | | |
| 79 | | | | |
| 80 | | | | |
| 81 | | | | |
| 82 | | | | |
| 83 | | | | |
| 84 | | | | |
| 85 | | | | |
| 86 | | | | |
| 87 | | | | |
| 88 | | | | |
| 89 | | | | |
| 90 | | | | |

# Feature ~ Difference

**Objective** _____

| | Target | | | |
|---|---|---|---|---|
| 1 | airplane/train – sky/tracks | | | |
| 2 | apple/banana – red/yellow | | | |
| 3 | banana/orange – yellow/orange | | | |
| 4 | boat/car – water/street | | | |
| 5 | book/video – read/watch | | | |
| 6 | car/motorcycle – 4 wheels/2 | | | |
| 7 | cat/dog – meow/woof | | | |
| 8 | ears/mouth – listen/talk | | | |
| 9 | elephant/mouse – big/small | | | |
| 10 | eyes/nose – see/smell | | | |
| 11 | hat/shoes – head/feet | | | |
| 12 | laugh/cry – happy/sad | | | |
| 13 | plate/cup – food/water | | | |
| 14 | rock/pillow – hard/soft | | | |
| 15 | sidewalk/street – people/cars | | | |
| 16 | sock/pants – foot/leg | | | |
| 17 | sun/moon – day/night | | | |
| 18 | tree/flower – big/small | | | |
| 19 | water/coffee - cold/hot | | | |
| 20 | winter/summer – cold/hot | | | |
| 21 | | | | |
| 22 | | | | |
| 23 | | | | |
| 24 | | | | |
| 25 | | | | |
| 26 | | | | |
| 27 | | | | |
| 28 | | | | |
| 29 | | | | |
| 30 | | | | |
| 31 | | | | |
| 32 | | | | |
| 33 | | | | |
| 34 | | | | |
| 35 | | | | |
| 36 | | | | |
| 37 | | | | |
| 38 | | | | |
| 39 | | | | |
| 40 | | | | |

# Feature ~ Likeness

**Objective** _____

| Target | | | |
|---|---|---|---|
| 1  banana/apple - fruit | | | |
| 2  bicycle/tricycle - wheels | | | |
| 3  car/truck - vehicles | | | |
| 4  cereal/eggs - breakfast | | | |
| 5  circle/square - shape | | | |
| 6  cookie/cake - sweet desert | | | |
| 7  cow/pig - farm animals | | | |
| 8  eyes/nose - face | | | |
| 9  giraffe/zebra - zoo animals | | | |
| 10  guitar/piano - instruments | | | |
| 11  hot dog/bacon - meat | | | |
| 12  juice/milk - drinks | | | |
| 13  legos/puzzles - toys | | | |
| 14  mom/dad - family | | | |
| 15  pants/shorts - wear on legs | | | |
| 16  pen/pencil - write with | | | |
| 17  penny/quarter - money | | | |
| 18  pretzel/potato chip - snacks | | | |
| 19  refrigerator/stove - kitchen | | | |
| 20  window/door - open | | | |
| 21 | | | |
| 22 | | | |
| 23 | | | |
| 24 | | | |
| 25 | | | |
| 26 | | | |
| 27 | | | |
| 28 | | | |
| 29 | | | |
| 30 | | | |
| 31 | | | |
| 32 | | | |
| 33 | | | |
| 34 | | | |
| 35 | | | |
| 36 | | | |
| 37 | | | |
| 38 | | | |
| 39 | | | |
| 40 | | | |

# Feature ~ Object

**Objective** _____

| Target | | | |
|---|---|---|---|
| 1  airplane has a pilot | | | |
| 2  airplane has a tail | | | |
| 3  airplane has wings | | | |
| 4  ambulance has a siren | | | |
| 5  ambulance is white | | | |
| 6  ant has antenae | | | |
| 7  ant has many legs | | | |
| 8  ant is small | | | |
| 9  apple has skin | | | |
| 10  apple is red | | | |
| 11  arm has elbow | | | |
| 12  arm has hand | | | |
| 13  backpack has a zipper | | | |
| 14  backpack has straps | | | |
| 15  bacon is brown | | | |
| 16  bacon is crunchy | | | |
| 17  bacon is greasy | | | |
| 18  balloon is filled with air | | | |
| 19  balloon is round | | | |
| 20  banana has a peel | | | |
| 21  banana is yellow | | | |
| 22  bandaid goes on a boo boo | | | |
| 23  bandaid is sticky | | | |
| 24  baseball is hard | | | |
| 25  baseball is white | | | |
| 26  baseball player has a glove | | | |
| 27  basketball goes in a hoop | | | |
| 28  basketball has black stripes | | | |
| 29  basketball is orange | | | |
| 30  bat is long | | | |
| 31  bat is made of wood | | | |
| 32  bathing suit is for swimming | | | |
| 33  bathtub has a drain | | | |
| 34  bathtub has a faucet | | | |
| 35  beach has sand | | | |
| 36  beach has water | | | |
| 37  bed has a blanket | | | |
| 38  bed has a pillow | | | |
| 39  bed has sheets | | | |
| 40  bee has wings | | | |

# Feature ~ Object

**Objective** _____

| Target | | | |
|---|---|---|---|
| 41  bees live in a hive | | | |
| 42  belt goes on your pants | | | |
| 43  belt has a buckle | | | |
| 44  belt is made of leather | | | |
| 45  bike has a seat | | | |
| 46  bike has handlebars | | | |
| 47  bike has pedals | | | |
| 48  bike has wheels | | | |
| 49  bird has a beak | | | |
| 50  bird has feathers | | | |
| 51  bird has wings | | | |
| 52  book has a cover | | | |
| 53  book has pages | | | |
| 54  book has pictures | | | |
| 55  book has words | | | |
| 56  broom has a handle | | | |
| 57  broom has bristles | | | |
| 58  brush has a handle | | | |
| 59  brush has bristles | | | |
| 60  butterfly has wings | | | |
| 61  butterfly is pretty | | | |
| 62  cake has candles | | | |
| 63  cake has frosting | | | |
| 64  cake is sweet | | | |
| 65  camera has buttons | | | |
| 66  camera has film | | | |
| 67  camera uses batteries | | | |
| 68  can opener has a sharp blade | | | |
| 69  can opener is metal | | | |
| 70  candle burns | | | |
| 71  candle is hot | | | |
| 72  candle is made of wax | | | |
| 73  car has a doors | | | |
| 74  car has a steering wheel | | | |
| 75  car has a trunk | | | |
| 76  car has wheels | | | |
| 77  carrots are crunchy | | | |
| 78  carrots are orange | | | |
| 79  carrots are sweet | | | |
| 80  cat has a tail | | | |

# Feature ~ Object

**Objective** _____

| | Target | | | |
|---|---|---|---|---|
| 81 | cat has whiskers | | | |
| 82 | cat is a pet | | | |
| 83 | cat is soft | | | |
| 84 | cd has games | | | |
| 85 | cd is flat | | | |
| 86 | cd is round | | | |
| 87 | cereal is crunchy | | | |
| 88 | cereal is for breakfast | | | |
| 89 | chair has a seat | | | |
| 90 | chair has back | | | |
| 91 | chair has legs | | | |
| 92 | chicken has feathers | | | |
| 93 | chips are crunchy | | | |
| 94 | chips are made from potatoes | | | |
| 95 | chips are salty | | | |
| 96 | chips come in a bag | | | |
| 97 | Christmas brings Santa Claus | | | |
| 98 | Christmas is a time for presents | | | |
| 99 | Christmas is in December | | | |
| 100 | clock has hands | | | |
| 101 | clock has numbers | | | |
| 102 | clouds are white | | | |
| 103 | clouds make rain | | | |
| 104 | coffee is a hot drink | | | |
| 105 | computer has a mouse | | | |
| 106 | computer is for playing games | | | |
| 107 | cookie sheet goes in the oven | | | |
| 108 | cookie sheet is flat | | | |
| 109 | cookie sheet is made of metal | | | |
| 110 | cookies are round | | | |
| 111 | cookies are sweet | | | |
| 112 | cow has udders | | | |
| 113 | crayon made of wax | | | |
| 114 | crayons are sharpened | | | |
| 115 | crayons come in many colors | | | |
| 116 | curtains made of cloth | | | |
| 117 | dinosaur lived many years ago | | | |
| 118 | dinosaurs are big | | | |
| 119 | dinosaurs had sharp teeth | | | |
| 120 | dishwasher needs soap | | | |

# Feature ~ Object

**Objective** _____

| Target | | | |
|---|---|---|---|
| 121 dog has 4 legs | | | |
| 122 dog has paws | | | |
| 123 duck has 2 feet | | | |
| 124 duck has a beak | | | |
| 125 duck has feathers | | | |
| 126 egg has a shell | | | |
| 127 egg has a yoke | | | |
| 128 egg is white | | | |
| 129 elephant has a trunk | | | |
| 130 elephant has big ears | | | |
| 131 elephant is grey | | | |
| 132 feet have toes | | | |
| 133 fence is metal | | | |
| 134 fingers have fingernails | | | |
| 135 fingers have knuckles | | | |
| 136 fire is hot | | | |
| 137 fire is red | | | |
| 138 fire makes smoke | | | |
| 139 fire truck has a ladder | | | |
| 140 fire truck has a siren | | | |
| 141 fire truck is red | | | |
| 142 fish has fins | | | |
| 143 fish has scales | | | |
| 144 fish has tail | | | |
| 145 flashlight is turned on/off | | | |
| 146 flashlight makes light | | | |
| 147 flashlight uses batteries | | | |
| 148 flower grows outside | | | |
| 149 flower has a stem | | | |
| 150 flower has petals | | | |
| 151 french fries are greasy | | | |
| 152 french fries are hot | | | |
| 153 french fries are made from potatoes | | | |
| 154 french fries are salty | | | |
| 155 frog has a long tongue | | | |
| 156 frog is green | | | |
| 157 frog is slimy | | | |
| 158 garden has dirt | | | |
| 159 glasses have lenses | | | |
| 160 glue is sticky | | | |

# Feature ~ Object

**Objective** _____

| | Target | | | |
|---|---|---|---|---|
| 161 | glue is white | | | |
| 162 | grass grows in the yard | | | |
| 163 | grass is green | | | |
| 164 | grass is on the ground | | | |
| 165 | grill gets hot | | | |
| 166 | grill is used outside | | | |
| 167 | guitar has strings | | | |
| 168 | guitar is something you play | | | |
| 169 | guitar made of wood | | | |
| 170 | guitar makes music | | | |
| 171 | hair gets brushed | | | |
| 172 | hair gets cut | | | |
| 173 | hair gets washed | | | |
| 174 | Halloween is for trick or treating | | | |
| 175 | Halloween is in October | | | |
| 176 | Halloween is when you get candy | | | |
| 177 | Halloween you wear a costume | | | |
| 178 | hammer has a metal head | | | |
| 179 | hammer has a wood handle | | | |
| 180 | hammer hits nails | | | |
| 181 | hand has fingers | | | |
| 182 | hand is a body part | | | |
| 183 | horse has a mane | | | |
| 184 | horse has a tail | | | |
| 185 | ice cream is cold | | | |
| 186 | ice cream is sweet | | | . |
| 187 | ice is cold | | | |
| 188 | juice is made from fruit | | | |
| 189 | juice is poured in a cup | | | |
| 190 | juice is sweet | | | |
| 191 | kangaroo has 2 legs | | | |
| 192 | kangaroo has a pouch | | | |
| 193 | key is made of metal | | | |
| 194 | key is on a key chain | | | |
| 195 | kite has a string | | | |
| 196 | kitten is a baby cat | | | |
| 197 | Kleenex comes in a box | | | |
| 198 | Kleenex is for blowing your nose | | | |
| 199 | Kleenex is made of paper | | | |
| 200 | knife has a handle | | | |

# Feature ~ Object

**Objective** _____

| Target | | | |
|---|---|---|---|
| 201 | knife is sharp | | | |
| 202 | lamp gets plugged in | | | |
| 203 | lamp has a light bulb | | | |
| 204 | lamp has a switch | | | |
| 205 | lawnmower has a blade | | | |
| 206 | lawnmower is noisy | | | |
| 207 | lawnmower uses gas | | | |
| 208 | leaf falls on the ground | | | |
| 209 | leaf grows on a tree | | | |
| 210 | leaf is green | | | |
| 211 | leg has a knee | | | |
| 212 | lettuce goes in salad | | | |
| 213 | lettuce is crunchy | | | |
| 214 | lettuce is green | | | |
| 215 | magazine has pages | | | |
| 216 | magazine has pictures | | | |
| 217 | magazine has stories | | | |
| 218 | marble is a small ball | | | |
| 219 | marble is round | | | |
| 220 | marshmallow is sweet | | | |
| 221 | marshmallow is white | | | |
| 222 | microwave has a door | | | |
| 223 | microwave has buttons | | | |
| 224 | milk is a cold drink | | | |
| 225 | milk is for cereal | | | |
| 226 | milk is kept in the refrigerator | | | |
| 227 | milk is white | | | |
| 228 | mirror is flat | | | |
| 229 | mirror is for looking at yourself | | | |
| 230 | mirror is shiny | | | |
| 231 | money has numbers on it | | | |
| 232 | money is for buying things | | | |
| 233 | monkey eats bananas | | | |
| 234 | monkey has a tail | | | |
| 235 | monkey lives in the jungle | | | |
| 236 | moon is big | | | |
| 237 | moon is bright | | | |
| 238 | moon is in the sky | | | |
| 239 | motorcycle has 2 wheels | | | |
| 240 | motorcycle has an engine | | | |

# Feature ~ Object

**Objective** _____

| | Target | | | |
|---|---|---|---|---|
| 241 | motorcycle has handlebars | | | |
| 242 | motorcycle uses gas | | | |
| 243 | nail clippers are sharp | | | |
| 244 | nail clippers cut your fingernails | | | |
| 245 | napkin is for your mouth | | | |
| 246 | napkin is made of paper | | | |
| 247 | newspaper has pictures | | | |
| 248 | newspaper has stories | | | |
| 249 | newspaper is made of paper | | | |
| 250 | orange grows on trees | | | |
| 251 | orange is juicy | | | |
| 252 | orange is orange | | | |
| 253 | orange is round | | | |
| 254 | oven has a door | | | |
| 255 | oven has buttons | | | |
| 256 | oven is hot | | | |
| 257 | owl has feathers | | | |
| 258 | owl has wings | | | |
| 259 | owl lives in a tree | | | |
| 260 | pants cover your legs | | | |
| 261 | pants have a zipper | | | |
| 262 | pants made of cloth | | | |
| 263 | paper is for writing | | | |
| 264 | paper is made from trees | | | |
| 265 | paper is white | | | |
| 266 | peas are a vegetable | | | |
| 267 | peas are green | | | |
| 268 | peas are small | | | |
| 269 | peas are sweet | | | |
| 270 | pen has ink | | | |
| 271 | pencil has an eraser | | | |
| 272 | pencil has lead | | | |
| 273 | piano has black and white keys | | | |
| 274 | piano makes music | | | |
| 275 | pig has a snout | | | |
| 276 | pig is fat | | | |
| 277 | pig lives on a farm | | | |
| 278 | pig stinks | | | |
| 279 | pizza has a crust | | | |
| 280 | pizza has cheese | | | |

# Feature ~ Object

**Objective** _____

| | Target | | | |
|---|---|---|---|---|
| 281 | pizza is round | | | |
| 282 | playdoh is soft | | | |
| 283 | playdoh is squishy | | | |
| 284 | pumpkin grows in a patch | | | |
| 285 | pumpkin has a stem | | | |
| 286 | pumpkin is orange | | | |
| 287 | puppy is a baby dog | | | |
| 288 | puzzle has pieces | | | |
| 289 | puzzle is made of wood | | | |
| 290 | quarter is metal | | | |
| 291 | quarter is money | | | |
| 292 | quarter is round | | | |
| 293 | quarter is silver | | | |
| 294 | rabbit eats carrots | | | |
| 295 | rabbit has a tail | | | |
| 296 | rabbit has long ears | | | |
| 297 | rain comes from clouds | | | |
| 298 | rain gets you wet | | | |
| 299 | rain makes puddles | | | |
| 300 | rainbow has many colors | | | |
| 301 | rainbow is in the sky | | | |
| 302 | refrigerator has a door | | | |
| 303 | refrigerator is cold | | | |
| 304 | room has a closet | | | |
| 305 | sandwich has bread | | | |
| 306 | sausage is brown | | | |
| 307 | sausage is greasy | | | |
| 308 | scissors are sharp | | | |
| 309 | scissors have a handle | | | |
| 310 | scissors have blades | | | |
| 311 | shampoo comes in a bottle | | | |
| 312 | shampoo makes bubbles | | | |
| 313 | shampoo used on your hair | | | |
| 314 | sheep is white | | | |
| 315 | sheep lives on a farm | | | |
| 316 | shirt has buttons | | | |
| 317 | shirt has sleeves | | | |
| 318 | shoes go on your feet | | | |
| 319 | shoes have laces | | | |
| 320 | sky is blue | | | |

# Feature ~ Object

**Objective** _____

| Target | | | |
|---|---|---|---|
| 321 slide has a ladder | | | |
| 322 slide is slippery | | | |
| 323 snake crawls on the ground | | | |
| 324 snake is long | | | |
| 325 snake is slimy | | | |
| 326 snow is cold | | | |
| 327 snow is white | | | |
| 328 soap makes bubbles | | | |
| 329 soccer ball gets kicked | | | |
| 330 soccer ball is black and white | | | |
| 331 socks come in pairs | | | |
| 332 socks go on your feet | | | |
| 333 soup goes in a bowl | | | |
| 334 soup is eaten with a spoon | | | |
| 335 soup is hot | | | |
| 336 stapler is made of metal | | | |
| 337 stapler used on paper | | | |
| 338 stapler uses staples | | | |
| 339 stereo has buttons | | | |
| 340 stereo has speakers | | | |
| 341 stereo plays music | | | |
| 342 stroller carries kids | | | |
| 343 stroller has a seat | | | |
| 344 stroller has wheels | | | |
| 345 sun is hot | | | |
| 346 sun is yellow | | | |
| 347 table has a top | | | |
| 348 table has legs | | | |
| 349 table is made of wood | | | |
| 350 tape helps wrap presents | | | |
| 351 tape holds things | | | |
| 352 tape is sticky | | | |
| 353 tape recorder gets plugged in | | | |
| 354 tape recorder has buttons | | | |
| 355 tape recorder plays tapes | | | |
| 356 Tarzan has brown hair | | | |
| 357 Tarzan is a man | | | |
| 358 telephone has a cord | | | |
| 359 telephone has a plug | | | |
| 360 telephone has buttons | | | |

# Feature ~ Object

**Objective:** _____

| | Target | | | |
|---|---|---|---|---|
| 361 | telephone has numbers | | | |
| 362 | tiger has a tail | | | |
| 363 | tiger has stripes | | | |
| 364 | tiger lives in the jungle | | | |
| 365 | towel is made of cloth | | | |
| 366 | towel is soft | | | |
| 367 | train has an engine | | | |
| 368 | train has an engineer | | | |
| 369 | train runs on tracks | | | |
| 370 | tree has a trunk | | | |
| 371 | tree has branches | | | |
| 372 | tree has leaves | | | |
| 373 | turkey has feathers | | | |
| 374 | turkey has wings | | | |
| 375 | turkey lives on a farm | | | |
| 376 | turtle has a little tail | | | |
| 377 | turtle has a shell | | | |
| 378 | TV has a screen | | | |
| 379 | TV has buttons | | | |
| 380 | TV uses a remote | | | |
| 381 | vacuum cleans up | | | |
| 382 | vacuum has a bag | | | |
| 383 | vacuum has a plug | | | |
| 384 | vacuum is noisy | | | |
| 385 | VCR gets rewound | | | |
| 386 | VCR goes with the TV | | | |
| 387 | VCR has buttons | | | |
| 388 | VCR plays videos | | | |
| 389 | video is black | | | |
| 390 | video is put in the VCR | | | |
| 391 | wheelbarrow has 2 wheels | | | |
| 392 | wheelbarrow has a handle | | | |
| 393 | wheelbarrow is used outside | | | |
| 394 | zebra has a tail | | | |
| 395 | zebra is black and white | | | |
| 396 | zebra lives at the zoo | | | |
| 397 | | | | |
| 398 | | | | |
| 399 | | | | |
| 400 | | | | |

# Feature ~ Place

**Objective:** _____

| | Target | | | |
|---|---|---|---|---|
| 1 | elevator has buttons | | | |
| 2 | elevator has doors | | | |
| 3 | elevator has numbers | | | |
| 4 | escalator has steps | | | |
| 5 | escalator is at the mall | | | |
| 6 | farm has a barn | | | |
| 7 | farm has a farmer | | | |
| 8 | farm has a tractor | | | |
| 9 | grocery store has food | | | |
| 10 | grocery store has shopping carts | | | |
| 11 | house has a door | | | |
| 12 | house has roof | | | |
| 13 | house has windows | | | |
| 14 | library has books | | | |
| 15 | library has CDs | | | |
| 16 | library has videos | | | |
| 17 | mall has an escalator | | | |
| 18 | mall has the Disney store | | | |
| 19 | McDonalds has a play land | | | |
| 20 | McDonalds has hamburgers | | | |
| 21 | McDonalds is a restaurant | | | |
| 22 | nest is in a tree | | | |
| 23 | nest is made of twigs | | | |
| 24 | nest is where birds live | | | |
| 25 | ocean has a beach | | | |
| 26 | ocean has fish | | | |
| 27 | ocean has water | | | |
| 28 | ocean has waves | | | |
| 29 | park has a slide | | | |
| 30 | park has a swing | | | |
| 31 | park has see saw | | | |
| 32 | pool has a ladder | | | |
| 33 | pool has diving board | | | |
| 34 | pool has water | | | |
| 35 | school bus has a driver | | | |
| 36 | school bus has wheels | | | |
| 37 | school bus is yellow | | | |
| 38 | tent has a zipper | | | |
| 39 | tent is for sleeping | | | |
| 40 | tent is used outside | | | |

Language Targets to Teach a Child to Communicate

# Function ~ Body

**Objective:** _____

| Target | | | |
|---|---|---|---|
| 1 arm – raise | | | |
| 2 bottom – sit on | | | |
| 3 ears – hear | | | |
| 4 ears – listen | | | |
| 5 eyes – blink | | | |
| 6 eyes – close | | | |
| 7 eyes – open | | | |
| 8 eyes – see | | | |
| 9 feet – jump | | | |
| 10 feet – stomp | | | |
| 11 feet – walk | | | |
| 12 fingernails – cut | | | |
| 13 hair – brush | | | |
| 14 hair – comb | | | |
| 15 hair – cut | | | |
| 16 hair – wash | | | |
| 17 hands – clap | | | |
| 18 hands – wash | | | |
| 19 knees – bend | | | |
| 20 mouth – eat | | | |
| 21 mouth – smile | | | |
| 22 mouth – talk | | | |
| 23 nose – blow | | | |
| 24 nose – sneeze | | | |
| 25 nose – snore | | | |
| 26 tongue – taste | | | |
| 27 | | | |
| 28 | | | |
| 29 | | | |
| 30 | | | |
| 31 | | | |
| 32 | | | |
| 33 | | | |
| 34 | | | |
| 35 | | | |
| 36 | | | |
| 37 | | | |
| 38 | | | |
| 39 | | | |
| 40 | | | |

# Function ~ Object

**Objective:** _____

| | Target | | | |
|----|-------------------------------------|--|--|--|
| 1 | airplane flies | | | |
| 2 | airplane lands | | | |
| 3 | airplane takes off | | | |
| 4 | ambulance carries sick people | | | |
| 5 | ambulance goes fast | | | |
| 6 | ant lives in dirt | | | |
| 7 | Arthur eats chocolate birthday cake | | | |
| 8 | Arthur plays computer games | | | |
| 9 | Arthur wears glasses | | | |
| 10 | baby cries | | | |
| 11 | baby sleeps in a crib | | | |
| 12 | baby wears diapers | | | |
| 13 | backpack gets zipped up | | | |
| 14 | backpack goes on your back | | | |
| 15 | backpack holds things | | | |
| 16 | ball bounces | | | |
| 17 | ball is for catching | | | |
| 18 | ball is kicked | | | |
| 19 | ball is thrown | | | |
| 20 | balloon floats in the sky | | | |
| 21 | balloon is blown up | | | |
| 22 | balloon pops | | | |
| 23 | banana is eaten | | | |
| 24 | banana is peeled | | | |
| 25 | baseball is hit with a bat | | | |
| 26 | baseball is played on a field | | | |
| 27 | baseball player - runs the bases | | | |
| 28 | baseball player swings a bat | | | |
| 29 | bat swings | | | |
| 30 | bathing suit gets wet | | | |
| 31 | bathtub fills with water | | | |
| 32 | bed is for sleeping in | | | |
| 33 | bees make honey | | | |
| 34 | bell rings | | | |
| 35 | bike is for riding | | | |
| 36 | bike is parked | | | |
| 37 | blanket covers the bed | | | |
| 38 | blanket keeps you warm | | | |
| 39 | book gets opened | | | |
| 40 | book has pages to turn | | | |

# Function ~ Object

**Objective:** _____

| Target | | | |
|---|---|---|---|
| 41 book is read | | | |
| 42 broom sweeps | | | |
| 43 bubbles are blown | | | |
| 44 bubbles pop | | | |
| 45 cake gets baked | | | |
| 46 cake gets frosting | | | |
| 47 cake is eaten at a birthday party | | | |
| 48 camera is smiled at | | | |
| 49 camera takes a picture | | | |
| 50 candles blow them out | | | |
| 51 candles light up | | | |
| 52 car gets parked | | | |
| 53 car is driven | | | |
| 54 car is something you ride in | | | |
| 55 clock tells times | | | |
| 56 clock ticks | | | |
| 57 coat gets hung up | | | |
| 58 coat gets put on | | | |
| 59 coat is taken take off | | | |
| 60 coat keeps you warm | | | |
| 61 computer gets turn on | | | |
| 62 computer gets turned off | | | |
| 63 computer lets you play games | | | |
| 64 cow makes milk | | | |
| 65 crayon gets peeled | | | |
| 66 crayon helps you draw | | | |
| 67 cup gets filled up | | | |
| 68 cup is used drink | | | |
| 69 curtains block out the sun | | | |
| 70 curtains hang on the window | | | |
| 71 dishes get dried | | | |
| 72 dishes get put away | | | |
| 73 dishes get washed | | | |
| 74 dishwasher cleans dishes | | | |
| 75 dog barks | | | |
| 76 dog gets fed | | | |
| 77 dog is pet | | | |
| 78 dog walks | | | |
| 79 door is opened | | | |
| 80 door is shut | | | |

# Function ~ Object

**Objective:** _____

| Target | | | |
|---|---|---|---|
| 81  drum gets pounded on | | | |
| 82  dryer drys clothes | | | |
| 83  dryer gets hot | | | |
| 84  duck swims in a pond | | | |
| 85  dump truck - carries dirt | | | |
| 86  fire burns | | | |
| 87  fire gets put out | | | |
| 88  fire gives light | | | |
| 89  flower blooms | | | |
| 90  flower get cut | | | |
| 91  flower gets smelled | | | |
| 92  fork is used to eat with | | | |
| 93  game is for playing | | | |
| 94  game is for taking turns | | | |
| 95  glass breaks | | | |
| 96  grass gets mowed | | | |
| 97  grill cooks meat | | | |
| 98  hat goes on your head | | | |
| 99  helicopter has propellers | | | |
| 100  hole gets filled up | | | |
| 101  hole is dug up | | | |
| 102  horse gets brush | | | |
| 103  horse gets fed | | | |
| 104  horse is for riding | | | |
| 105  house is where people live | | | |
| 106  ice cream melts | | | |
| 107  ice cream tastes good | | | |
| 108  key locks door | | | |
| 109  key opens the door | | | |
| 110  kite flies | | | |
| 111  kite uses a string | | | |
| 112  knife cuts | | | |
| 113  knot gets tied | | | |
| 114  knot gets untied | | | |
| 115  ladder is climbed | | | |
| 116  light gets turn off | | | |
| 117  light gets turned on | | | |
| 118  marble rolls | | | |
| 119  microwave beeps | | | |
| 120  microwave cooks food | | | |

# Function ~ Object

**Objective:** _____

| Target | | | |
|---|---|---|---|
| 121 milk pours on cereal | | | |
| 122 necklace is worn around your neck | | | |
| 123 oven bakes food | | | |
| 124 oven feels hot | | | |
| 125 pan helps you cook food | | | |
| 126 pants get zipped | | | |
| 127 pants snap | | | |
| 128 paper is something you write on | | | |
| 129 paper rips | | | |
| 130 pencil helps you write | | | |
| 131 pencil is sharpened | | | |
| 132 picture gets drawn | | | |
| 133 picture gets taken | | | |
| 134 plants need water | | | |
| 135 pool is for splashing in | | | |
| 136 pool is for swimming | | | |
| 137 present is unwrapped | | | |
| 138 refrigerator gets its door opened | | | |
| 139 refrigerator keeps food cold | | | |
| 140 school bus carries children | | | |
| 141 scissors cut paper | | | |
| 142 seatbelt is worn in the car | | | |
| 143 shampoo is used to wash hair | | | |
| 144 shampoo make lather | | | |
| 145 shirt is buttoned | | | |
| 146 shirt is something to wear | | | |
| 147 shoes get put on | | | |
| 148 shoes get tied | | | |
| 149 shovel is something you dig with | | | |
| 150 soap is for washing | | | |
| 151 soccer ball gets thrown | | | |
| 152 soccer ball is kicked | | | |
| 153 song is sung | | | |
| 154 spoon is used to eat | | | |
| 155 spoon stirs | | | |
| 156 store is somewhere you go | | | |
| 157 store is wear you shop | | | |
| 158 sun goes down | | | |
| 159 sun shines | | | |
| 160 swing is pushed | | | |

# Function ~ Object

**Objective:** _____

| | Target | | | |
|---|---|---|---|---|
| 161 | table is for sitting at | | | |
| 162 | table is somewhere to put food | | | |
| 163 | Tarzan eats meat | | | |
| 164 | Tarzan says whoo whoo | | | |
| 165 | Tarzan swings in trees | | | |
| 166 | teeth get brushed | | | |
| 167 | teeth gets flossed | | | |
| 168 | telephone is something to talk on | | | |
| 169 | telephone rings | | | |
| 170 | television gets turned on | | | |
| 171 | television is watched | | | |
| 172 | towel is used to dry off | | | |
| 173 | towel is used to wipe | | | |
| 174 | toys are to play with | | | |
| 175 | toys get cleaned up | | | |
| 176 | trash can is for throwing away | | | |
| 177 | umbrella gets opened up | | | |
| 178 | umbrella stops the rain | | | |
| 179 | | | | |
| 180 | | | | |
| 181 | | | | |
| 182 | | | | |
| 183 | | | | |
| 184 | | | | |
| 185 | | | | |
| 186 | | | | |
| 187 | | | | |
| 188 | | | | |
| 189 | | | | |
| 190 | | | | |
| 191 | | | | |
| 192 | | | | |
| 193 | | | | |
| 194 | | | | |
| 195 | | | | |
| 196 | | | | |
| 197 | | | | |
| 198 | | | | |
| 199 | | | | |
| 200 | | | | |

# Function ~ Place

**Objective:** _____

| Target | | | |
|---|---|---|---|
| 1  airport - fly a plane | | | |
| 2  ballpit - jump in the balls | | | |
| 3  bank - get money | | | |
| 4  barn - animals sleep | | | |
| 5  book store - buy books | | | |
| 6  car wash - clean the car | | | |
| 7  carnival - play games | | | |
| 8  church - pray | | | |
| 9  farm - see farm animals | | | |
| 10  gas station - get gas | | | |
| 11  grocery store - buy food | | | |
| 12  harbor - park boats | | | |
| 13  hospital - get better | | | |
| 14  library - get books | | | |
| 15  mall - go shopping | | | |
| 16  motel - sleep | | | |
| 17  path - walk | | | |
| 18  playground - slide | | | |
| 19  pool - swim | | | |
| 20  post office - mail letter | | | |
| 21  restaurant - eat food | | | |
| 22  store - go shopping | | | |
| 23  tennis court - play tennis | | | |
| 24  theater - see movie | | | |
| 25  train station - ride the train | | | |
| 26  waiting room - sit and wait | | | |
| 27  zoo - see animals | | | |
| 28 | | | |
| 29 | | | |
| 30 | | | |
| 31 | | | |
| 32 | | | |
| 33 | | | |
| 34 | | | |
| 35 | | | |
| 36 | | | |
| 37 | | | |
| 38 | | | |
| 39 | | | |
| 40 | | | |

# Function ~ Room

**Objective:** _____

| | Target | | | |
|---|---|---|---|---|
| 1 | basement - store things | | | |
| 2 | bathroom - go potty | | | |
| 3 | bedroom - sleep | | | |
| 4 | dining room - eat | | | |
| 5 | family room - watch TV | | | |
| 6 | garage - park car | | | |
| 7 | kitchen - cook | | | |
| 8 | laundry room - clean clothes | | | |
| 9 | living room - sit | | | |
| 10 | pantry - get food | | | |
| 11 | | | | |
| 12 | | | | |
| 13 | | | | |
| 14 | | | | |
| 15 | | | | |
| 16 | | | | |
| 17 | | | | |
| 18 | | | | |
| 19 | | | | |
| 20 | | | | |
| 21 | | | | |
| 22 | | | | |
| 23 | | | | |
| 24 | | | | |
| 25 | | | | |
| 26 | | | | |
| 27 | | | | |
| 28 | | | | |
| 29 | | | | |
| 30 | | | | |
| 31 | | | | |
| 32 | | | | |
| 33 | | | | |
| 34 | | | | |
| 35 | | | | |
| 36 | | | | |
| 37 | | | | |
| 38 | | | | |
| 39 | | | | |
| 40 | | | | |

## Chapter 8 - Phrase

# Adjective + Noun

Objective: _____

| | Target | | | |
|---|---|---|---|---|
| 1 | cold ice cream | | | |
| 2 | cold water | | | |
| 3 | crunchy snack | | | |
| 4 | hot coffee | | | |
| 5 | lemon tree | | | |
| 6 | orange tree | | | |
| 7 | pretty flower | | | |
| 8 | salty french fries | | | |
| 9 | salty snack | | | |
| 10 | soft marshmallow | | | |
| 11 | sour lemon | | | |
| 12 | sticky candy | | | |
| 13 | sweet cookie | | | |
| 14 | sweet treat | | | |
| 15 | | | | |
| 16 | | | | |
| 17 | | | | |
| 18 | | | | |
| 19 | | | | |
| 20 | | | | |

# Adjective + Adjective + Noun

Objective: _____

| | Target | | | |
|---|---|---|---|---|
| 1 | big black animal | | | |
| 2 | big black bear | | | |
| 3 | big blue balloon | | | |
| 4 | big brown bat | | | |
| 5 | big green backpack | | | |
| 6 | big grey animal | | | |
| 7 | big grey castle | | | |
| 8 | big grey elephant | | | |
| 9 | big orange pumpkin | | | |
| 10 | cold breakfast cereal | | | |
| 11 | cold breakfast food | | | |
| 12 | cold strawberry desert | | | |

# Adjective + Adjective + Noun

**Objective:** _____

| | Target | | | |
|---|---|---|---|---|
| 13 | cold strawberry ice cream | | | |
| 14 | crispy green celery | | | |
| 15 | crispy green food | | | |
| 16 | cute little animal | | | |
| 17 | cute little puppy | | | |
| 18 | four orange basketballs | | | |
| 19 | hot salty □rench fries | | | |
| 20 | little black spider | | | |
| 21 | little green frog | | | |
| 22 | little red car | | | |
| 23 | little white egg | | | |
| 24 | little yellow ball | | | |
| 25 | salty crunchy chips | | | |
| 26 | scary black spider | | | |
| 27 | small crunchy snack | | | |
| 28 | three chocolate cakes | | | |
| 29 | three red hearts | | | |
| 30 | three yellow bananas | | | |
| 31 | two red apples | | | |

# Article + Adjective + Noun

**Objective:** _____

| | Target | | | |
|---|---|---|---|---|
| 1 | a blue one | | | |
| 2 | the big one | | | |
| 3 | the red one | | | |
| 4 | the sweet one | | | |

# Article + Noun

**Objective:** _____

| | Target | | | |
|---|---|---|---|---|
| 1 | a car | | | |
| 2 | a cookie | | | |
| 3 | a dollhouse | | | |
| 4 | the airplane | | | |
| 5 | the dog | | | |

# Attention + Noun

**Objective:** _____

| Target | | | |
|---|---|---|---|
| 1 bye dad | | | |
| 2 hi mom | | | |
| 3 look car | | | |
| 4 that airplane | | | |
| 5 | | | |

# Color + Noun

**Objective:** _____

| Target | | | |
|---|---|---|---|
| 1 black candy | | | |
| 2 blue airplane | | | |
| 3 brown cat | | | |
| 4 green fish | | | |
| 5 grey truck | | | |
| 6 orange cat | | | |
| 7 pink crayon | | | |
| 8 purple house | | | |
| 9 red strawberry | | | |
| 10 white sock | | | |
| 11 yellow flowers | | | |
| 12 | | | |
| 13 | | | |

# Disappearance

**Objective:** _____

| Target | | | |
|---|---|---|---|
| 1 banana all gone | | | |
| 2 cookie all gone | | | |
| 3 daddy all gone | | | |
| 4 mommy bye bye | | | |
| 5 toy missing | | | |
| 6 | | | |
| 7 | | | |
| 8 | | | |

# Leader Phrase

**Objective:** _____

| Target | | | |
|---|---|---|---|
| 1 | I found a | | | |
| 2 | I got a | | | |
| 3 | I have a | | | |
| 4 | I hear a | | | |
| 5 | I need a | | | |
| 6 | I see a | | | |
| 7 | I smell a | | | |
| 8 | I use a | | | |
| 9 | I want a | | | |
| 10 | It has | | | |
| 11 | May I have | | | |
| 12 | That is a | | | |
| 13 | There is | | | |

# Negation

**Objective:** _____

| Target | | | |
|---|---|---|---|
| 1 | no bath | | | |
| 2 | no bye bye | | | |
| 3 | no drink | | | |
| 4 | no go | | | |
| 5 | no sleep | | | |

# Noun + Location

**Objective:** _____

| Target | | | |
|---|---|---|---|
| 1 | apples in box | | | |
| 2 | cat in basket | | | |
| 3 | crayon on table | | | |
| 4 | girl up stairs | | | |
| 5 | hat on head | | | |
| 6 | horse in barn | | | |
| 7 | orangutan in tree | | | |
| 8 | thumbs up | | | |
| 9 | tongue out | | | |
| 10 | train on track | | | |

Language Targets to Teach a Child to Communicate

# Number + Noun

**Objective:** _____

| Target | | | |
|---|---|---|---|
| 1 four fingers | | | |
| 2 four triangles | | | |
| 3 one chair | | | |
| 4 one cookie | | | |
| 5 three bananas | | | |
| 6 three carrots | | | |
| 7 three trains | | | |
| 8 two blocks | | | |
| 9 two circles | | | |
| 10 two forks | | | |

# Of Phrase

**Objective:** _____

| Target | | | |
|---|---|---|---|
| 1 bag of chips | | | |
| 2 bag of popcorn | | | |
| 3 bag of pretzels | | | |
| 4 bag of toys | | | |
| 5 bar of soap | | | |
| 6 bottle of pills | | | |
| 7 bowl of cereal | | | |
| 8 box of cereal | | | |
| 9 box of crackers | | | |
| 10 bunch of grapes | | | |
| 11 bunch of toys | | | |
| 12 can of soda | | | |
| 13 can of soup | | | |
| 14 carton of milk | | | |
| 15 glass of milk | | | |
| 16 head of lettuce | | | |
| 17 loaf of bread | | | |
| 18 pack of gum | | | |
| 19 pair of boots | | | |
| 20 pair of earrings | | | |
| 21 pair of pants | | | |
| 22 pair of shoes | | | |
| 23 pair of skates | | | |
| 24 pair of socks | | | |
| 25 piece of bacon | | | |

# Of Phrase

**Objective:** _____

| | Target | | | |
|---|---|---|---|---|
| 26 | piece of cake | | | |
| 27 | scoop of ice cream | | | |
| 28 | sheet of paper | | | |
| 29 | slice of bread | | | |
| 30 | stick of butter | | | |
| 31 | stick of gum | | | |
| 32 | tube of toothpaste | | | |

# Possessor + Possession

**Objective:** _____

| | Target | | | |
|---|---|---|---|---|
| 1 | aladdin's castle | | | |
| 2 | baby's bottle | | | |
| 3 | king's crown | | | |
| 4 | mom's car | | | |
| 5 | his shoes | | | |
| 6 | my truck | | | |
| 7 | pirate's hat | | | |
| 8 | Sleeping Beauty's castle | | | |
| 9 | woody's hat | | | |

# Preposition + Noun

**Objective:** _____

| | Target | | | |
|---|---|---|---|---|
| 1 | behind the curtain | | | |
| 2 | in the basket | | | |
| 3 | in the box | | | |
| 4 | off the couch | | | |
| 5 | on the couch | | | |
| 6 | out of the basket | | | |
| 7 | out of the box | | | |
| 8 | over the hill | | | |
| 9 | under the chair | | | |
| 10 | up the stairs | | | |

# Pronoun + Verb

**Objective:** _____

| Target | | | |
|---|---|---|---|
| 1  he drinks | | | |
| 2  he eats | | | |
| 3  he sits | | | |
| 4  I eat | | | |
| 5  I take | | | |
| 6  I want | | | |
| 7  she climbs | | | |
| 8  she rides | | | |
| 9  they run | | | |
| 10  we go | | | |
| 11 | | | |
| 12 | | | |
| 13 | | | |
| 14 | | | |
| 15 | | | |

# Recurrence

**Objective:** _____

| Target | | | |
|---|---|---|---|
| 1  blow again | | | |
| 2  do again | | | |
| 3  eat more | | | |
| 4  go again | | | |
| 5  more candy | | | |
| 6  more music | | | |
| 7  more please | | | |
| 8  one more push | | | |
| 9 | | | |
| 10 | | | |
| 11 | | | |
| 12 | | | |
| 13 | | | |
| 14 | | | |
| 15 | | | |

# Sequence

**Objective:** _____

| | Target | | | |
|---|---|---|---|---|
| 1 | bedtime 1 – take a bath | | | |
| 2 | bedtime 2 – dry off with a towel | | | |
| 3 | bedtime 3 – put on pajamas | | | |
| 4 | bedtime 4 – brush teeth | | | |
| 5 | bedtime 5 – go to the bathroom | | | |
| 6 | bedtime 6 – get in bed | | | |
| 7 | bedtime 7 – read a book | | | |
| 8 | bedtime 8 – pull up the covers | | | |
| 9 | bedtime 9 – turn off light | | | |
| 10 | bedtime 10 – close eyes | | | |
| 11 | bedtime 11 – go to sleep | | | |
| 12 | brush teeth 1 – get toothbrush | | | |
| 13 | brush teeth 2 – get toothpaste | | | |
| 14 | brush teeth 3 – get toothbrush wet | | | |
| 15 | brush teeth 4 – put on toothpaste | | | |
| 16 | brush teeth 5 – brush teeth | | | |
| 17 | brush teeth 6 – spit out toothpaste | | | |
| 18 | brush teeth 7 – rinse toothbrush | | | |
| 19 | camping 1 – go to the forest | | | |
| 20 | camping 2 – put up tent | | | |
| 21 | camping 3 – have a campfire | | | |
| 22 | camping 4 – get in sleeping bad | | | |
| 23 | camping 5 – go to sleep under moon | | | |
| 24 | car ride 1 – get in the car | | | |
| 25 | car ride 2 – put on seatbelt | | | |
| 26 | car ride 3 – drive car | | | |
| 27 | computer 1 – turn on | | | |
| 28 | computer 2 – put in CD | | | |
| 29 | computer 3 – play game | | | |
| 30 | dentist 1 – sit in chair | | | |
| 31 | dentist 2 – clean teeth | | | |
| 32 | dentist 3 – watch movie | | | |
| 33 | dentist 4 – get a prize | | | |
| 34 | dressed 1 – put on underwear | | | |
| 35 | dressed 2 – put on pants | | | |
| 36 | dressed 3 – put on shirt | | | |
| 37 | dressed 4 – put on socks | | | |
| 38 | dressed 5 – put on shoes | | | |
| 39 | dressed 6 – put on coat | | | |

# Sequence

**Objective:** _____

| Target | | | |
|---|---|---|---|
| 40 Halloween 1 – put on costume | | | |
| 41 Halloween 2 – go to house | | | |
| 42 Halloween 3 – knock on door | | | |
| 43 Halloween 4 – say trick or treat | | | |
| 44 Halloween 5 – get candy | | | |
| 45 Halloween 6 – say thank you | | | |
| 46 library 1 – go to the library | | | |
| 47 library 2 – go to the door | | | |
| 48 library 3 – open the door | | | |
| 49 library 4 – find a book | | | |
| 50 library 5 – get in line | | | |
| 51 library 6 – get libaray card ready | | | |
| 52 library 7 – check out books | | | |
| 53 library 8 – pay late fines | | | |
| 54 muffins 1 – get ingredients | | | |
| 55 muffins 2 – mix the batter | | | |
| 56 muffins 3 – put in muffin tin | | | |
| 57 muffins 4 – put in the oven | | | |
| 58 muffins 5 – take out of the oven | | | |
| 59 muffins 6 – eat muffins | | | |
| 60 plant 1 – plant a seed | | | |
| 61 plant 2 – water the seed | | | |
| 62 plant 3 – watch it grow | | | |
| 63 slide 1 – climb up | | | |
| 64 slide 2 – ready to go | | | |
| 65 slide 3 – slide down | | | |
| 66 snowman 1 – make bottom | | | |
| 67 snowman 2 – make middle | | | |
| 68 snowman 3 – make head | | | |
| 69 snowman 4 – make the hat | | | |
| 70 snowman 5 – make the face | | | |
| 71 snowman 6- make the arms | | | |
| 72 swing 1 – get on the swing | | | |
| 73 swing 2 – get a push | | | |
| 74 swing 3 -  say whee | | | |
| 75 wash hands 1 – go to the sink | | | |
| 76 wash hands 2 – turn on the water | | | |
| 77 wash hands 3 – get the soap | | | |
| 78 wash hands 4 – wash hands | | | |
| 79 wash hands 5 -- rinse hands | | | |
| 80 wash hands 6 -- dry off | | | |

# Size + Noun

**Objective:** _____

| | Target | | | |
|---|---|---|---|---|
| 1 | big fire truck | | | |
| 2 | big piano | | | |
| 3 | big Pooh | | | |
| 4 | big train | | | |
| 5 | little mouse | | | |
| 6 | little piano | | | |
| 7 | little Pooh | | | |
| 8 | little train | | | |
| 9 | small marshmallow | | | |
| 10 | tall giraffe | | | |

# Verb + Noun

**Objective:** _____

| | Target | | | |
|---|---|---|---|---|
| 1 | brush dog | | | |
| 2 | brush hair | | | |
| 3 | brush teeth | | | |
| 4 | carry bag | | | |
| 5 | carry box | | | |
| 6 | carry shoes | | | |
| 7 | clean fingernails | | | |
| 8 | clean table | | | |
| 9 | clean window | | | |
| 10 | close book | | | |
| 11 | close box | | | |
| 12 | close container | | | |
| 13 | close door | | | |
| 14 | cook bacon | | | |
| 15 | cook meat | | | |
| 16 | cook muffins | | | |
| 17 | cover bed | | | |
| 18 | cover box | | | |
| 19 | cover doll | | | |
| 20 | draw circle | | | |
| 21 | draw face | | | |
| 22 | draw snowman | | | |
| 23 | dress baby | | | |

# Verb + Noun

**Objective:** _____

| Target | | | |
|---|---|---|---|
| 24 dress boy | | | |
| 25 dress doll | | | |
| 26 drop ball | | | |
| 27 drop block | | | |
| 28 drop book | | | |
| 29 dry dishes | | | |
| 30 dry face | | | |
| 31 dry hands | | | |
| 32 eat banana | | | |
| 33 eat cookie | | | |
| 34 eat muffin | | | |
| 35 feed baby | | | |
| 36 feed cat | | | |
| 37 feed horse | | | |
| 38 fix car | | | |
| 39 fix that | | | |
| 40 fix toy | | | |
| 41 get ball | | | |
| 42 get box | | | |
| 43 get Tarzan | | | |
| 44 give coat | | | |
| 45 give drink | | | |
| 46 give socks | | | |
| 47 go to bathroom | | | |
| 48 go to kitchen | | | |
| 49 go to park | | | |
| 50 hit ball | | | |
| 51 hit balloon | | | |
| 52 hit table | | | |
| 53 hold baby | | | |
| 54 hold rabbit | | | |
| 55 hold umbrella | | | |
| 56 jump down | | | |
| 57 jump fence | | | |
| 58 jump rope | | | |
| 59 kick ball | | | |
| 60 kick floor | | | |
| 61 kick wall | | | |
| 62 open box | | | |
| 63 open container | | | |
| 64 open door | | | |

# Verb + Noun

**Objective:** _____

| | Target | | | |
|---|---|---|---|---|
| 65 | open refrigerator | | | |
| 66 | paint fingers | | | |
| 67 | paint picture | | | |
| 68 | paint wall | | | |
| 69 | peel apple | | | |
| 70 | peel banana | | | |
| 71 | peel orange | | | |
| 72 | pet cat | | | |
| 73 | pet dog | | | |
| 74 | pet hamster | | | |
| 75 | pinch arm | | | |
| 76 | pinch leg | | | |
| 77 | pinch nose | | | |
| 78 | play cards | | | |
| 79 | play cars | | | |
| 80 | play cash register | | | |
| 81 | play computer | | | |
| 82 | play drum | | | |
| 83 | play game | | | |
| 84 | play guitar | | | |
| 85 | play kitchen | | | |
| 86 | play piano | | | |
| 87 | play with beads | | | |
| 88 | point to door | | | |
| 89 | point to house | | | |
| 90 | point to oven | | | |
| 91 | pour juice | | | |
| 92 | pour milk | | | |
| 93 | pour tea | | | |
| 94 | pull chair | | | |
| 95 | pull train | | | |
| 96 | pull wagon | | | |
| 97 | push box | | | |
| 98 | push swing | | | |
| 99 | push wagon | | | |
| 100 | put in candy | | | |
| 101 | put in cookie | | | |
| 102 | put in money | | | |
| 103 | put on coat | | | |
| 104 | put on shirt | | | |
| 105 | put on shoes | | | |

# Verb + Noun

**Objective:** _____

| | Target | | | |
|---|---|---|---|---|
| 106 | raise hand | | | |
| 107 | read book | | | |
| 108 | read map | | | |
| 109 | read paper | | | |
| 110 | ride bike | | | |
| 111 | ride horse | | | |
| 112 | ride train | | | |
| 113 | scratch arm | | | |
| 114 | scratch head | | | |
| 115 | scratch leg | | | |
| 116 | shake hand | | | |
| 117 | shake head | | | |
| 118 | shake tambourine | | | |
| 119 | sit on chair | | | |
| 120 | sit on couch | | | |
| 121 | sit on floor | | | |
| 122 | smell bacon | | | |
| 123 | smell chocolate | | | |
| 124 | smell flower | | | |
| 125 | take off coat | | | |
| 126 | take off hat | | | |
| 127 | take off shoes | | | |
| 128 | throw ball | | | |
| 129 | throw bat | | | |
| 130 | throw leaves | | | |
| 131 | touch feet | | | |
| 132 | touch head | | | |
| 133 | touch nose | | | |
| 134 | wash face | | | |
| 135 | wash hands | | | |
| 136 | water flower | | | |
| 137 | water grass | | | |
| 138 | water plant | | | |
| 139 | wipe nose | | | |
| 140 | wipe table | | | |
| 141 | wipe window | | | |
| 142 | | | | |
| 143 | | | | |
| 144 | | | | |
| 145 | | | | |
| 146 | | | | |

# Verb + Preposition

**Objective:** _____

| | Target | | | |
|---|---|---|---|---|
| 1 | climb up | | | |
| 2 | fall down | | | |
| 3 | fly above | | | |
| 4 | go under | | | |
| 5 | hide behind | | | |
| 6 | jump over | | | |
| 7 | look below | | | |
| 8 | sit down | | | |
| 9 | swim through | | | |
| 10 | throw up | | | |
| 11 | | | | |
| 12 | | | | |
| 13 | | | | |
| 14 | | | | |
| 15 | | | | |
| 16 | | | | |
| 17 | | | | |
| 18 | | | | |
| 19 | | | | |
| 20 | | | | |
| 21 | | | | |
| 22 | | | | |
| 23 | | | | |
| 24 | | | | |
| 25 | | | | |
| 26 | | | | |
| 27 | | | | |
| 28 | | | | |
| 29 | | | | |
| 30 | | | | |
| 31 | | | | |
| 32 | | | | |
| 33 | | | | |
| 34 | | | | |
| 35 | | | | |
| 36 | | | | |
| 37 | | | | |
| 38 | | | | |
| 39 | | | | |
| 40 | | | | |

## Chapter 9 - Question

# Question ~ Academic

Objective: _____

| | Target | | | |
|---|---|---|---|---|
| 1 | What are some bodies of water? | | | |
| 2 | What are some city name? | | | |
| 3 | What are some coins? | | | |
| 4 | What are some community helpers? | | | |
| 5 | What are some continents? | | | |
| 6 | What are some dinosaurs? | | | |
| 7 | What are some forest plants? | | | |
| 8 | What are some habitats? | | | |
| 9 | What are some holiday? | | | |
| 10 | What are some planets? | | | |
| 11 | What are some natural disasters? | | | |
| 12 | What are some states? | | | |
| 13 | What are some traffic signs? | | | |
| 14 | What are the days of the week? | | | |
| 15 | What are the months of the year? | | | |
| 16 | What are the seasons? | | | |
| 17 | What are types of weather? | | | |
| 18 | What are water animals? | | | |
| 19 | Where are land forms? | | | |
| 20 | Where are places to live? | | | |
| 21 | Who is in a family? | | | |
| 22 | Who is the president? | | | |
| 23 | Who were the first people in America? | | | |
| 24 | Who works at the post office? | | | |
| 25 | Who works in a hospital? | | | |
| 26 | | | | |
| 27 | | | | |
| 28 | | | | |
| 29 | | | | |
| 30 | | | | |
| 31 | | | | |
| 32 | | | | |
| 33 | | | | |
| 34 | | | | |
| 35 | | | | |
| 36 | | | | |
| 37 | | | | |
| 38 | | | | |
| 39 | | | | |
| 40 | | | | |

# Question ~ Asks

**Objective:** _____

| | Target | | | |
|---|---|---|---|---|
| 1 | Are those your toys? | | | |
| 2 | Are you ok? | | | |
| 3 | Can I go? | | | |
| 4 | Can I play? | | | |
| 5 | Can I stay? | | | |
| 6 | Can I take a break? | | | |
| 7 | Do you want this? | | | |
| 8 | Does this one fit? | | | |
| 9 | Does this one work? | | | |
| 10 | How are you? | | | |
| 11 | How do you do it? | | | |
| 12 | How does it work? | | | |
| 13 | How many are there? | | | |
| 14 | Is there a show on? | | | |
| 15 | Is this your cup? | | | |
| 16 | May I have a turn? | | | |
| 17 | May I have that? | | | |
| 18 | May I have a __? | | | |
| 19 | What are you doing? | | | |
| 20 | What color? | | | |
| 21 | What did you do? | | | |
| 22 | What did you say? | | | |
| 23 | What did you see? | | | |
| 24 | What do you do with this? | | | |
| 25 | What do you drink? | | | |
| 26 | What do you eat? | | | |
| 27 | What do you have? | | | |
| 28 | What do you like? | | | |
| 29 | What do you want? | | | |
| 30 | What does he eat? | | | |
| 31 | What does he say? | | | |
| 32 | What happened? | | | |
| 33 | What is it? | | | |
| 34 | What is that? | | | |
| 35 | What is this for? | | | |
| 36 | What is your dog's name? | | | |
| 37 | What should I do? | | | |
| 38 | What time is it? | | | |
| 39 | What's he doing? | | | |
| 40 | What's in the box? | | | |

Language Targets to Teach a Child to Communicate

# Question ~ Asks

**Objective:** _____

| Target | | | |
|---|---|---|---|
| 41 | What's on TV? | | | |
| 42 | What's wrong? | | | |
| 43 | When can I go? | | | |
| 44 | When can I have that? | | | |
| 45 | Where are the ____? | | | |
| 46 | Where are you going? | | | |
| 47 | Where are you? | | | |
| 48 | Where can I get more of these? | | | |
| 49 | Where did it go? | | | |
| 50 | Where did you go? | | | |
| 51 | Where do you find it? | | | |
| 52 | Where do you put this? | | | |
| 53 | Where does he live? | | | |
| 54 | Where is ____? | | | |
| 55 | Where is he? | | | |
| 56 | Where is it? | | | |
| 57 | Which one can I have? | | | |
| 58 | Which one is mine? | | | |
| 59 | Which one? | | | |
| 60 | Who has it? | | | |
| 61 | Who has the ____? | | | |
| 62 | Who is that? | | | |
| 63 | Who uses this? | | | |
| 64 | Who's there? | | | |
| 65 | Whose is this? | | | |
| 66 | Whose turn is it? | | | |
| 67 | Why do I have to? | | | |
| 68 | Why does it work? | | | |
| 69 | Why? | | | |
| 70 | Will you fix this? | | | |
| 71 | | | | |
| 72 | | | | |
| 73 | | | | |
| 74 | | | | |
| 75 | | | | |
| 76 | | | | |
| 77 | | | | |
| 78 | | | | |
| 79 | | | | |
| 80 | | | | |

# Question ~ Community

**Objective:** _____

| | Target | | | |
|---|---|---|---|---|
| 1 | Do you walk in the road? | | | |
| 2 | What do you do at Target? | | | |
| 3 | What do you at the gas station? | | | |
| 4 | What do you do at Costco? | | | |
| 5 | What do you get at Blockbusters? | | | |
| 6 | What do you see at the airport? | | | |
| 7 | What happens at a fire? | | | |
| 8 | What is at play land? | | | |
| 9 | What is at the beach? | | | |
| 10 | What is at the grocery store? | | | |
| 11 | What is at the library? | | | |
| 12 | What is at the park? | | | |
| 13 | What is at the post office? | | | |
| 14 | What is in the backyard? | | | |
| 15 | What is in the forest? | | | |
| 16 | What restaurant do you go to? | | | |
| 17 | Where do you like to go? | | | |
| 18 | Where does mail go? | | | |
| 19 | Where is your school? | | | |
| 20 | Who is at the fire station? | | | |
| 21 | Who is at the police station? | | | |
| 22 | Who is in your neighborhood? | | | |
| 23 | | | | |
| 24 | | | | |
| 25 | | | | |
| 26 | | | | |
| 27 | | | | |
| 28 | | | | |
| 29 | | | | |
| 30 | | | | |
| 31 | | | | |
| 32 | | | | |
| 33 | | | | |
| 34 | | | | |
| 35 | | | | |
| 36 | | | | |
| 37 | | | | |
| 38 | | | | |
| 39 | | | | |
| 40 | | | | |

# Question ~ Current Events

**Objective:** _____

| | Target | | | |
|---|---|---|---|---|
| 1 | How is the weather? | | | |
| 2 | What are you watching? | | | |
| 3 | What do you do at a Birthday party? | | | |
| 4 | What do you do at Halloween? | | | |
| 5 | What do you do at night time? | | | |
| 6 | What do you do at Thanksgiving? | | | |
| 7 | What do you do in the afternoon? | | | |
| 8 | What do you do in the morning? | | | |
| 9 | What do you do in the snow? | | | |
| 10 | What do you do on Sunday? | | | |
| 11 | What do you see at school? | | | |
| 12 | What happens at a baseball game? | | | |
| 13 | What happens at Easter? | | | |
| 14 | What happens on Christmas? | | | |
| 15 | What happens on New Years eve? | | | |
| 16 | What happens on the 4th of July? | | | |
| 17 | | | | |
| 18 | | | | |
| 19 | | | | |
| 20 | | | | |

# Question ~ How

**Objective:** _____

| | Target | | | |
|---|---|---|---|---|
| 1 | How do birds fly? | | | |
| 2 | How do you blow out candles? | | | |
| 3 | How do you bounce a ball? | | | |
| 4 | How do you brush your teeth? | | | |
| 5 | How do you buy things? | | | |
| 6 | How do you check out a library book? | | | |
| 7 | How do you comb your hair? | | | |
| 8 | How do you cook food? | | | |
| 9 | How do you cut meat? | | | |
| 10 | How do you cut paper? | | | |
| 11 | How do you cut wood? | | | |
| 12 | How do you draw a face? | | | |
| 13 | How do you dry your hair? | | | |
| 14 | How do you dry your hands? | | | |

# Question ~ How

**Objective:** _____

| | Target | | | |
|---|---|---|---|---|
| 15 | How do you eat a banana? | | | |
| 16 | How do you eat an orange? | | | |
| 17 | How do you eat cereal? | | | |
| 18 | How do you eat dinner? | | | |
| 19 | How do you fly a kite? | | | |
| 20 | How do you get dressed? | | | |
| 21 | How do you get to school? | | | |
| 22 | How do you glue things together? | | | |
| 23 | How do you go down a slide? | | | |
| 24 | How do you go swimming? | | | |
| 25 | How do you go to sleep? | | | |
| 26 | How do you go up a slide? | | | |
| 27 | How do you hit a nail? | | | |
| 28 | How do you keep your hands warm? | | | |
| 29 | How do you keep your head warm? | | | |
| 30 | How do you kick a ball? | | | |
| 31 | How do you mail a letter? | | | |
| 32 | How do you make a sand castle? | | | |
| 33 | How do you make a sandwich? | | | |
| 34 | How do you make applesauce? | | | |
| 35 | How do you measure something? | | | |
| 36 | How do you open a present? | | | |
| 37 | How do you play a drum? | | | |
| 38 | How do you play a guitar? | | | |
| 39 | How do you play the piano? | | | |
| 40 | How do you put on shoes? | | | |
| 41 | How do you ride a bike? | | | |
| 42 | How do you stop the rain on your head? | | | |
| 43 | How do you take a bath? | | | |
| 44 | How do you tell time? | | | |
| 45 | How do you trim your nails? | | | |
| 46 | How do you unlock the door? | | | |
| 47 | How do you wash your hair? | | | |
| 48 | How do you wash your hands? | | | |
| 49 | How do you watch TV? | | | |
| 50 | How do you jump? | | | |
| 51 | How do you talk quietly? | | | |
| 52 | | | | |
| 53 | | | | |
| 54 | | | | |

# Question ~ Personal Events

**Objective:** _____

| Target | | | |
|---|---|---|---|
| 1  What did you do at school? | | | |
| 2  What did you do yesterday? | | | |
| 3  What did you eat for breakfast? | | | |
| 4  What do you do at the beach? | | | |
| 5  What do you wear to school? | | | |
| 6  What do you like to eat? | | | |
| 7  What do you want for Christmas? | | | |
| 8  What do you want for your birthday? | | | |
| 9  What will you be for Halloween? | | | |
| 10  Where do you play? | | | |

# Question ~ Reciprocal

**Objective:** _____

| Target | | | |
|---|---|---|---|
| 1  How are you feeling? | | | |
| 2  How do you do it? | | | |
| 3  How does your food taste? | | | |
| 4  What did you do today? | | | |
| 5  What do you like? | | | |
| 6  What do you want to play with? | | | |
| 7  What color do you want? | | | |
| 8  What's your favorite game? | | | |
| 9  Where did you go? | | | |
| 10  Where do you like to go? | | | |
| 11  Which one do you want? | | | |
| 12  Which one is yours? | | | |
| 13 | | | |
| 14 | | | |
| 15 | | | |
| 16 | | | |
| 17 | | | |
| 18 | | | |
| 19 | | | |
| 20 | | | |

# Question ~ Social

**Objective:** _____

| Target | | | |
|---|---|---|---|
| 1  Do you have a bike? | | | |
| 2  Do you have a brother? | | | |
| 3  Do you have a pet? | | | |
| 4  Do you have a sister? | | | |
| 5  Do you like brocolli? | | | |
| 6  Do you like candy? | | | |
| 7  Do you want this one or that one? | | | |
| 8  Do you wear glasses? | | | |
| 9  How are you doing? | | | |
| 10  How old are you? | | | |
| 11  What are you going to do? | | | |
| 12  What are you playing with? | | | |
| 13  What are your eating? | | | |
| 14  What color are your eyes? | | | |
| 15  What color is mom's car? | | | |
| 16  What color is your hair? | | | |
| 17  What do you have to play with? | | | |
| 18  What do you like to do? | | | |
| 19  What do you like to drink? | | | |
| 20  What do you like to eat? | | | |
| 21  What is your address? | | | |
| 22  What is your favorite book? | | | |
| 23  What is your favorite movie? | | | |
| 24  What is your last name? | | | |
| 25  What is your name? | | | |
| 26  What is your pet? | | | |
| 27  What is your phone number? | | | |
| 28  When is your birthday? | | | |
| 29  Where do you go to school? | | | |
| 30  Where do you live? | | | |
| 31  Where were you born? | | | |
| 32  Who cuts your hair? | | | |
| 33  Who is your brother? | | | |
| 34  Who is your dad? | | | |
| 35  Who is your friend? | | | |
| 36  Who is your mom? | | | |
| 37  Who is your neighbor? | | | |
| 38  Who is your sister? | | | |
| 39  Who is your teacher? | | | |

# Question ~ When

**Objective:** _____

| Target | | | |
|---|---|---|---|
| 1  When do flowers bloom? – in spring | | | |
| 2  When do leaves turn color? – in the fall | | | |
| 3  When do you answer the phone? – it rings | | | |
| 4  When do you bleed? – get a cut | | | |
| 5  When do you clean up? – done playing | | | |
| 6  When do you close your eyes? – sleep | | | |
| 7  When do you comb your hair? – messy | | | |
| 8  When do you cover your mouth? – cough | | | |
| 9  When do you cry? – sad | | | |
| 10  When do you decorate a tree? – Christmas | | | |
| 11  When do you drink? – thirsty | | | |
| 12  When do you dry off? – after a bath | | | |
| 13  When do you eat breakfast? – morning | | | |
| 14  When do you eat dinner? – night time | | | |
| 15  When do you eat? – hungry | | | |
| 16  When do you fly a kite? – its windy | | | |
| 17  When do you get dressed? – naked | | | |
| 18  When do you get quiet? – to listen | | | |
| 19  When do you go to the beach? – summer | | | |
| 20  When do you go to the doctor? – when sick | | | |
| 21  When do you hurry? – late | | | |
| 22  When do you laugh? – get tickled | | | |
| 23  When do you laugh? – something is funny | | | |
| 24  When do you need a bowl? – eat cereal | | | |
| 25  When do you need a broom? – sweep floor | | | |
| 26  When do you need a mop? – wash the floor | | | |
| 27  When do you open the door? – go outside | | | |
| 28  When do you put on bandaid? – cut skin | | | |
| 29  When do you put on socks? – feet are cold | | | |
| 30  When do you say goodbye? – leave | | | |
| 31  When do you say hello? – meet someone | | | |
| 32  When do you say please? – ask for things | | | |
| 33  When do you scratch? – itchy | | | |
| 34  When do you sit down? – tired of standing | | | |
| 35  When do you sleep? – tired | | | |
| 36  When do you smile? – happy | | | |
| 37  When do you snore? – sleep | | | |
| 38  When do you splash? -  in then water | | | |
| 39  When do you take a bath? – at night time | | | |
| 40  When do you take medicine? – your sick | | | |

# Question ~ When

**Objective:** _____

| | Target | | | |
|---|---|---|---|---|
| 41 | When do you turn on light? – its dark | | | |
| 42 | When do you turn on the fan? – too hot | | | |
| 43 | When do you turn the pages? – read a book | | | |
| 44 | When do you use a hairdryer? – hair is wet | | | |
| 45 | When do you use a key? – door is locked | | | |
| 46 | When do you use a shovel? – to dig | | | |
| 47 | When do you use a tissue? – blow nose | | | |
| 48 | When do you use an umbrella? – rains | | | |
| 49 | When do you use blocks? – to build a tower | | | |
| 50 | When do you use scissors? – to cut paper | | | |
| 51 | When do you use shampoo? – hair is dirty | | | |
| 52 | When do you wake up? – morning | | | |
| 53 | When do you wash? – dirty | | | |
| 54 | When do you water the grass? – need a hose | | | |
| 55 | When do you wear a coat? – its cold | | | |
| 56 | When do you wear a costume? – Halloween | | | |
| 57 | When do you wear a seatbelt? – ride in car | | | |
| 58 | When do you wear sunglasses? – sunny out | | | |
| 59 | When do you yell? – angry | | | |
| 60 | When does it get dark? – at night | | | |
| 61 | When does it snow? – in winter | | | |
| 62 | When does the sun come up? – morning | | | |
| 63 | When does your hair blow? - its windy | | | |
| 64 | When is your birthday? | | | |
| 65 | | | | |
| 66 | | | | |
| 67 | | | | |
| 68 | | | | |
| 69 | | | | |
| 70 | | | | |
| 71 | | | | |
| 72 | | | | |
| 73 | | | | |
| 74 | | | | |
| 75 | | | | |
| 76 | | | | |
| 77 | | | | |
| 78 | | | | |
| 79 | | | | |
| 80 | | | | |

# Question ~ Where

**Objective:** _____

| | Target | | | |
|---|---|---|---|---|
| 1 | Where are handlebars? - bike | | | |
| 2 | Where are the clouds? - sky | | | |
| 3 | Where are the stars? - sky | | | |
| 4 | Where are your fingers? - hand | | | |
| 5 | Where are your pillows? - bed | | | |
| 6 | Where do airplanes land? - airport | | | |
| 7 | Where do ants live? - dirt | | | |
| 8 | Where do cars drive? - traffic | | | |
| 9 | Where do fish live? - water | | | |
| 10 | Where do monkeys live? - jungle | | | |
| 11 | Where do oranges grow? - orange tree | | | |
| 12 | Where do people play golf? - golf course | | | |
| 13 | Where do people pray? - church | | | |
| 14 | Where do people ski? - on snow | | | |
| 15 | Where do pumpkins grow? - pumpkin patch | | | |
| 16 | Where do trains stop? - train station | | | |
| 17 | Where do you bake muffins? - oven | | | |
| 18 | Where do you borrow books? - library | | | |
| 19 | Where do you build a snowman? - snow | | | |
| 20 | Where do you buy books? - bookstore | | | |
| 21 | Where do you buy food? - grocery store | | | |
| 22 | Where do you buy fries? - McDonalds | | | |
| 23 | Where do you buy shoes? - shoe store | | | |
| 24 | Where do you buy toys? - toy store | | | |
| 25 | Where do you cook dinner? - kitchen | | | |
| 26 | Where do you eat food? - kitchen | | | |
| 27 | Where do you find a bed? - bedroom | | | |
| 28 | Where do you find a blanket? - bed | | | |
| 29 | Where do you find a roof? - house | | | |
| 30 | Where do you find a stove? - kitchen | | | |
| 31 | Where do you find a toilet? - bathroom | | | |
| 32 | Where do you find hair? - head | | | |
| 33 | Where do you find sand? - beach | | | |
| 34 | Where do you find the can opener? - kitchen | | | |
| 35 | Where do you find wings? - bird | | | |
| 36 | Where do fire engines park? - fire station | | | |
| 37 | Where do you get gas? - gas station | | | |
| 38 | Where do you get mail? - mailbox | | | |
| 39 | Where do you get money? - bank | | | |
| 40 | Where do you get sunburned? - in the sun | | | |

# Question ~ Where

**Objective:** _____

| | Target | | | |
|---|---|---|---|---|
| 41 | Where do you go down the slide? - park | | | |
| 42 | Where do you go out to eat? - restaurant | | | |
| 43 | Where do you go shopping? - store | | | |
| 44 | Where do you go to school? - school name | | | |
| 45 | Where do you have a zipper? - coat | | | |
| 46 | Where do you jump in the water? - pool | | | |
| 47 | Where do you keep a hamster? - cage | | | |
| 48 | Where do you keep eggs? - refrigerator | | | |
| 49 | Where do you keep food cold? - refrigerator | | | |
| 50 | Where do you keep your bicycle? - garage | | | |
| 51 | Where do you live? - name town | | | |
| 52 | Where do you make a snowman? - snow | | | |
| 53 | Where do you park a car? - garage | | | |
| 54 | Where do you play computer? -  office | | | |
| 55 | Where do you play in the sand? - sand box | | | |
| 56 | Where do you swing and slide? - playground | | | |
| 57 | Where do you put a CD? - computer | | | |
| 58 | Where do you put a video? - VCR | | | |
| 59 | Where do you put cheese? - pizza | | | |
| 60 | Where do you put chocolate chips? - cookies | | | |
| 61 | Where do you put coffee? - mug | | | |
| 62 | Where do you put dirty clothes? - washer | | | |
| 63 | Where do you put leash? - dog | | | |
| 64 | Where do you put mail? - mailbox | | | |
| 65 | Where do you put raisins? - muffins | | | |
| 66 | Where do you put shampoo? - hair | | | |
| 67 | Where do you put your coat? - closet | | | |
| 68 | Where do you put your head? - on a pillow | | | |
| 69 | Where do you run around? - park | | | |
| 70 | Where do you sit? - chair | | | |
| 71 | Where do you sleep? - bed | | | |
| 72 | Where do you stay on vacation? - motel | | | |
| 73 | Where do you swim? - pool | | | |
| 74 | Where do you take a bath? - bathtub | | | |
| 75 | Where do you take a walk? - outside | | | |
| 76 | Where do you use a lawn mower? - grass | | | |
| 77 | Where do you use a tent? - forest | | | |
| 78 | Where do you warm up food? - microwave | | | |
| 79 | Where do you wash your hands? - sink | | | |
| 80 | Where do you wear a hat? - head | | | |

# Question ~ Where

**Objective:** _____

| Target | | | |
|---|---|---|---|
| 81 Where do you wear a seatbelt? - car | | | |
| 82 Where do you wear glasses? - eyes | | | |
| 83 Where do you wear pants? - legs | | | |
| 84 Where do you work? - in the office | | | |
| 85 Where does a bird sleep? - nest | | | |
| 86 Where does a cow live? - farm | | | |
| 87 Where does a dog live? - house | | | |
| 88 Where does a frog live? - pond | | | |
| 89 Where does a horse sleep? - barn | | | |
| 90 Where does a lion live? - zoo | | | |
| 91 Where does an astronaut go? - space | | | |
| 92 Where does an elephant live? - zoo | | | |
| 93 Where does daylight come from? - sun | | | |
| 94 Where does it snow? - outside | | | |
| 95 Where does Pooh live? - 100 acre wood | | | |
| 96 Where does Tarzan live? - jungle | | | |
| 97 Where is the dishwasher? - kitchen | | | |
| 98 Where is the dryer? - laundry room | | | |
| 99 Where is the oven? - kitchen | | | |
| 100 Where is the refrigerator? - kitchen | | | |
| 101 Where is the shower? - bathroom | | | |
| 102 Where is the sink? - bathroom | | | |
| 103 Where is the TV? - family room | | | |
| 104 Where is your belly button? - belly | | | |
| 105 Where is your ear? - head | | | |
| 106 Where is your hair? - head | | | |
| 107 Where is your hand? - arm | | | |
| 108 Where is your knee? - leg | | | |
| 109 Where is your nose? - face | | | |
| 110 Where is your toothbrush? - bathroom | | | |
| 111 | | | |
| 112 | | | |
| 113 | | | |
| 114 | | | |
| 115 | | | |
| 116 | | | |
| 117 | | | |
| 118 | | | |
| 119 | | | |
| 120 | | | |

# Question ~ Which

**Objective:** _____

| Target | | | |
|---|---|---|---|
| 1 Which is a food? – cake or tree | | | |
| 2 Which is a plant? – tree or shoe | | | |
| 3 Which is an animal? – dog or book | | | |
| 4 Which is an insect? - butterfly or train | | | |
| 5 Which is big? – elephant or mouse | | | |
| 6 Which is blue? – sky or stars | | | |
| 7 Which is cold? – snow or scissors | | | |
| 8 Which is green? – grass or dirt | | | |
| 9 Which is hot? – sun or snow | | | |
| 10 Which is little? – bug or cow | | | |
| 11 Which is pretty? – flower or dirt | | | |
| 12 Which is salty? – chips or cake | | | |
| 13 Which is sour? – lemon or cookie | | | |
| 14 Which is sweet? – candy or chips | | | |
| 15 Which is wet? – water or car | | | |
| 16 Which is white? – cloud or grass | | | |
| 17 Which comes in a bunch? – grapes or meat | | | |
| 18 Which one cries? – baby or pencil | | | |
| 19 Which one do you blow? – bubbles or tape | | | |
| 20 Which one do you catch? – ball or couch | | | |
| 21 Which one do you clean up? – room or shoe | | | |
| 22 Which one do you crack? – egg or chair | | | |
| 23 Which do you drink from? – cup or plate | | | |
| 24 Which one do you eat with? – mouth or legs | | | |
| 25 Which one do you eat? – cookie or chair | | | |
| 26 Which one do you fly in? – airplane or train | | | |
| 27 Which do you hear with? – ears or hands | | | |
| 28 Which one do you kick with? – foot or hand | | | |
| 29 Which do you live in? – house or computer | | | |
| 30 Which one do you look in? – mirror or ball | | | |
| 31 Which do you peel? – banana or hot dog | | | |
| 32 Which one do you play? – piano or pants | | | |
| 33 Which one do you push? – wagon or house | | | |
| 34 Which do you put in the VCR?– video/book | | | |
| 35 Which one do you read? – book or camera | | | |
| 36 Which one do you ride? – bike or chair | | | |
| 37 Which one do you see with? – eyes or feet | | | |
| 38 Which one do you sit on? – chair or TV | | | |
| 39 Which do you sleep in? – bed or bathtub | | | |
| 40 Which one do you smell with? – nose or hair | | | |

# Question ~ Which

**Objective:** _____

| Target | | | |
|---|---|---|---|
| 41 Which one do you swim in? – pool or sink | | | |
| 42 Which do you touch with? – hands or knees | | | |
| 43 Which one do you turn on? – TV or book | | | |
| 44 Which do you wash in? – bathtub or oven | | | |
| 45 Which one do you watch? – TV or pencil | | | |
| 46 Which one do you wear? – shoes or bed | | | |
| 47 Which one eats? – cow or bike | | | |
| 48 Which one has leaves? – tree or grass | | | |
| 49 Which one has pages? – book or video | | | |
| 50 Which one writes? – pencil or scissors | | | |

# Question ~ Who

**Objective:** _____

| Target | | | |
|---|---|---|---|
| 1 Who builds a house? - carpenter | | | |
| 2 Who catches fish? - fisherman | | | |
| 3 Who cleans up? - janitor | | | |
| 4 Who cleans your teeth? - dentist | | | |
| 5 Who cooks food? - chef | | | |
| 6 Who cries? - baby | | | |
| 7 Who cuts meat? - butcher | | | |
| 8 Who dances? - dancer | | | |
| 9 Who delivers mail? - mailman | | | |
| 10 Who do you play with? - kids | | | |
| 11 Who drives a boat? - sailor | | | |
| 12 Who drives a bus? - bus driver | | | |
| 13 Who drives a train? - conductor | | | |
| 14 Who eats bananas? - monkey | | | |
| 15 Who eats grass? - horse | | | |
| 16 Who eats green eggs and ham? - Sam I am | | | |
| 17 Who eats honey? - Pooh | | | |
| 18 Who fights crime? - policeman | | | |
| 19 Who fights fires? - firefighter | | | |
| 20 Who fixes cars? - mechanic | | | |
| 21 Who fixes pipes? - plumber | | | |
| 22 Who flies an airplane? - pilot | | | |
| 23 Who flies in space? - astronaut | | | |
| 24 Who flies? – bird | | | |

# Question ~ Who

**Objective:** _____

| | Target | | | |
|---|---|---|---|---|
| 25 | Who guards the pool? - lifeguard | | | |
| 26 | Who has a long tail? - monkey | | | |
| 27 | Who has big ears? - elephant | | | |
| 28 | Who has black stripes? - zebra | | | |
| 29 | Who has long neck? - giraffe | | | |
| 30 | Who has whiskers? - cat | | | |
| 31 | Who helps people? - policeman | | | |
| 32 | Who helps you at the library? - librarian | | | |
| 33 | Who helps you when your sick? - doctor | | | |
| 34 | Who hops? - bunny | | | |
| 35 | Who is a bear? - Pooh | | | |
| 36 | Who is a big animal? - elephant | | | |
| 37 | Who is a boy? - Christopher Robin | | | |
| 38 | Who is a bug? - spider | | | |
| 39 | Who is a cowboy? - Woody | | | |
| 40 | Who is a Disney character? - Mickey Mouse | | | |
| 41 | Who is a dog? - Spot | | | |
| 42 | Who is a dwarf? - Sneezy | | | |
| 43 | Who is a girl? - Madeline | | | |
| 44 | Who is a jungle man? - Tarzan | | | |
| 45 | Who is a little animal? - rabbit | | | |
| 46 | Who is a man? - Dad | | | |
| 47 | Who is a princess? - Snow White | | | |
| 48 | Who is a purple dinosaur? - Barney | | | |
| 49 | Who is a woman? - Mom | | | |
| 50 | Who is Arthur's friend? - Buster | | | |
| 51 | Who is Arthur's puppy? - Pal | | | |
| 52 | Who is Arthur's sister? - D.W. | | | |
| 53 | Who is Buzz's friend? - Woody | | | |
| 54 | Who is D.W.'s brother? - Arthur | | | |
| 55 | Who is in Toy Story? - Woody | | | |
| 56 | Who is Piglet's friend? - Pooh | | | |
| 57 | Who is scary? - monster | | | |
| 58 | Who juggles balls? - juggler | | | |
| 59 | Who jumps? - frog | | | |
| 60 | Who kicks the ball? - soccer player | | | |
| 61 | Who leads circle time? - teacher | | | |
| 62 | Who lives in a castle? - king | | | |
| 63 | Who lives in a teepee? - Indian | | | |
| 64 | Who lives in an igloo? – Eskimo | | | |
| 65 | Who lives in the White House? – president | | | |

# Question ~ Who

**Objective:** _____

| Target | | | |
|--------|--|--|--|
| 66 Who lives next door? – neighbor | | | |
| 67 Who makes you laugh? - clown | | | |
| 68 Who plants food? - farmer | | | |
| 69 Who plays baseball? - baseball player | | | |
| 70 Who plays basketball? - basketball player | | | |
| 71 Who plays music? - musician | | | |
| 72 Who pulls a wagon? - horse | | | |
| 73 Who purrs? - cat | | | |
| 74 Who rides a broom? - witch | | | |
| 75 Who rides a horse? - cowboy | | | |
| 76 Who sleeps in baby bears bed? - goldilocks | | | |
| 77 Who stinks? - skunk | | | |
| 78 Who swims in the water? - fish | | | |
| 79 Who swings a bat? - baseball player | | | |
| 80 Who takes the garbage? - garbage man | | | |
| 81 Who teaches school? - teacher | | | |
| 82 Who throws a football?  - football player | | | |
| 83 Who watches kids? - babysitter | | | |
| 84 Who wears a crown? - king | | | |
| 85 Who works at a restaurant? - waitress | | | |
| 86 Who works at the store? - cashier | | | |

# Question ~ Why

**Objective:** _____

| Target | | | |
|--------|--|--|--|
| 1 Why do babies cry? | | | |
| 2 Why do you brush your teeth? | | | |
| 3 Why do you button a shirt? | | | |
| 4 Why do you cook food? | | | |
| 5 Why do you cover your mouth to cough? | | | |
| 6 Why do you drink water? | | | |
| 7 Why do you drive a car? | | | |
| 8 Why do you eat cake? | | | |
| 9 Why do you eat food? | | | |
| 10 Why do you get gas? | | | |
| 11 Why do you go to a restaurant? | | | |
| 12 Why do you go to school? | | | |
| 13 Why do you go to the doctor? | | | |

# Question ~ Why

**Objective:** _____

| | Target | | | |
|---|---|---|---|---|
| 14 | Why do you go to the zoo? | | | |
| 15 | Why do you peel a banana? | | | |
| 16 | Why do you put away playdoh? | | | |
| 17 | Why do you put cereal in a bowl? | | | |
| 18 | Why do you raise your hand? | | | |
| 19 | Why do you sleep? | | | |
| 20 | Why do you stop at a red light? | | | |
| 21 | Why do you tie a string on a balloon? | | | |
| 22 | Why do you use a backpack? | | | |
| 23 | Why do you use a blanket? | | | |
| 24 | Why do you use a fishing pole? | | | |
| 25 | Why do you use a knife? | | | |
| 26 | Why do you use a ladder? | | | |
| 27 | Why do you use a napkin? | | | |
| 28 | Why do you use a pencil? | | | |
| 29 | Why do you use a telephone? | | | |
| 30 | Why do you use a tissue? | | | |
| 31 | Why do you use a towel? | | | |
| 32 | Why do you use a wash machine? | | | |
| 33 | Why do you use an umbrella? | | | |
| 34 | Why do you use ice? | | | |
| 35 | Why do you use inside voices? | | | |
| 36 | Why do you use lights? | | | |
| 37 | Why do you use silverware? | | | |
| 38 | Why do you use soap? | | | |
| 39 | Why do you use the stairs? | | | |
| 40 | Why do you walk by the pool? | | | |
| 41 | Why do you wash your hands? | | | |
| 42 | Why do you water plants? | | | |
| 43 | Why do you wear a bathing suit? | | | |
| 44 | Why do you wear a coat? | | | |
| 45 | Why do you wear a watch? | | | |
| 46 | Why do you wear boots? | | | |
| 47 | Why do you wear glasses? | | | |
| 48 | Why do you wear sandals? | | | |
| 49 | Why does a building have a door? | | | |
| 50 | Why does a house have a window? | | | |
| 51 | | | | |
| 52 | | | | |
| 53 | | | | |
| 54 | | | | |

# Question ~ What is wrong?

**Objective:** _____

| Target | | | |
|---|---|---|---|
| 1  face has no eyes | | | |
| 2  drink from the wrong side of a cup | | | |
| 3  eat from wrong end of fork | | | |
| 4  girl has 2 noses | | | |
| 5  pants are on backwards | | | |
| 6  person has a tail | | | |
| 7  shirt is on your legs | | | |
| 8  shoe is on the wrong foot | | | |
| 9  wear a hat on your hand | | | |
| 10 wear mittens on your feet | | | |

# Question ~ Yes/No

**Objective:** _____

| Target | | | |
|---|---|---|---|
| 1  Can a fish sleep in a bed? | | | |
| 2  Can a fish swim? | | | |
| 3  Can a horse say neigh? | | | |
| 4  Can a horse sit in a chair? | | | |
| 5  Can a lion roar? | | | |
| 6  Can a lion take a shower? | | | |
| 7  Can a zebra brush his teeth? | | | |
| 8  Can a zebra run? | | | |
| 9  Can cows eat grass? | | | |
| 10 Can cows fly? | | | |
| 11 Do you bounce a ball? | | | |
| 12 Do you bounce a glass? | | | |
| 13 Do you buy food at the grocery store? | | | |
| 14 Do you buy food at the library? | | | |
| 15 Do you eat a ball? | | | |
| 16 Do you eat cookies? | | | |
| 17 Do you get bananas at McDonalds? | | | |
| 18 Do you get books at the library? | | | |
| 19 Do you get books in the garage? | | | |
| 20 Do you get fries at McDonalds? | | | |
| 21 Do you like to watch the dirt? | | | |
| 22 Do you like to watch videos? | | | |
| 23 Does a bus carry people? | | | |
| 24 Does a bus say woof woof? | | | |

# Question ~ Yes/No

**Objective:** _____

| | Target | | | |
|---|---|---|---|---|
| 25 | Does a car drive on the road? | | | |
| 26 | Does a car swim? | | | |
| 27 | Does a pillow go in the refrigerator? | | | |
| 28 | Does a pillow go on your bed? | | | |
| 29 | Does a sheep say ba ba? | | | |
| 30 | Does a sheep say moo? | | | |
| 31 | Does a shoe eat a cookie? | | | |
| 32 | Does a shoe go on your foot? | | | |
| 33 | Does a tree grow? | | | |
| 34 | Does a tree sing? | | | |
| 35 | Is a cookie dry? | | | |
| 36 | Is a cookie wet? | | | |
| 37 | Is a french fry salty? | | | |
| 38 | Is a french fry sweet? | | | |
| 39 | Is a spider an insect? | | | |
| 40 | Is a spider furniture? | | | |
| 41 | Is an elephant big? | | | |
| 42 | Is an elephant small? | | | |
| 43 | Is an ice cream cold? | | | |
| 44 | Is an ice cream hot? | | | |
| 45 | Will a house drive on the road? | | | |
| 46 | Will a house have a bathroom? | | | |
| 47 | Will a lion fly? | | | |
| 48 | Will a lion run? | | | |
| 49 | Will a pig dance? | | | |
| 50 | Will a pig say oink oink? | | | |
| 51 | Will you eat a box? | | | |
| 52 | Will you eat cereal? | | | |
| 53 | Will you sleep in a bed? | | | |
| 54 | Will you sleep in the pool? | | | |
| 55 | Will you wear a coat? | | | |
| 56 | Will you wear a refrigerator? | | | |
| 57 | | | | |
| 58 | | | | |
| 59 | | | | |
| 60 | | | | |
| 61 | | | | |
| 62 | | | | |
| 63 | | | | |
| 64 | | | | |

# Chapter 10 - Sentence Structure
## Sentence ~ I + Verb + Noun

Objective: _____

| Target | | | |
|---|---|---|---|
| 1 | I am a boy. | | | |
| 2 | I can read. | | | |
| 3 | I drink water | | | |
| 4 | I eat cookies. | | | |
| 5 | I go to school. | | | |
| 6 | I have blue eyes. | | | |
| 7 | I have brown hair. | | | |
| 8 | I hear an airplane. | | | |
| 9 | I like trains. | | | |
| 10 | I like to play computer games. | | | |
| 11 | I live in a house. | | | |
| 12 | I need a crayon. | | | |
| 13 | I play the piano. | | | |
| 14 | I dropped the book. | | | |
| 15 | I ride in a car. | | | |
| 16 | I see the cat. | | | |
| 17 | I smell a flower. | | | |
| 18 | I use a toothbrush. | | | |
| 19 | I want a hot dog. | | | |
| 20 | I wear shoes. | | | |
| 21 | | | | |
| 22 | | | | |
| 23 | | | | |
| 24 | | | | |
| 25 | | | | |

## Sentence ~ Pronoun + Be + Adjective

Objective: _____

| Target | | | |
|---|---|---|---|
| 1 | He is busy. | | | |
| 2 | He is noisy. | | | |
| 3 | He is tall. | | | |
| 4 | It is broken. | | | |
| 5 | It is small. | | | |
| 6 | She is happy. | | | |
| 7 | She was tired. | | | |
| 8 | They are quiet. | | | |

# Sentence ~ Sentence Stem

**Objective:** _____

| Target | | | |
|---|---|---|---|
| 1  Can I | | | |
| 2  He is | | | |
| 3  It is | | | |
| 4  She is | | | |
| 5  That's a | | | |
| 6  The boy is | | | |
| 7  The girl is | | | |
| 8  The kids are | | | |
| 9  The man is | | | |
| 10  The people are | | | |
| 11  They are | | | |
| 12  We are | | | |
| 13  You are | | | |
| 14  You have | | | |
| 15  | | | |
| 16  | | | |
| 17  | | | |
| 18  | | | |
| 19  | | | |
| 20  | | | |

# Sentence ~ Subject + Adverb + Verb + Object

**Objective:** _____

| Target | | | |
|---|---|---|---|
| 1  I always go home. | | | |
| 2  I never brush my hair. | | | |
| 3  I sometimes skip desert. | | | |
| 4  I usually brush my teeth. | | | |
| 5  | | | |
| 6  | | | |
| 7  | | | |
| 8  | | | |
| 9  | | | |
| 10  | | | |

# Sentence ~ Subject + Be + Adjective

**Objective:** _____

| Target | | | |
|---|---|---|---|
| 1  The car is red | | | |
| 2  The chips are salty. | | | |
| 3  The cookie is sweet. | | | |
| 4  The elephant is big. | | | |
| 5  The giraffe is tall. | | | |
| 6 | | | |
| 7 | | | |
| 8 | | | |
| 9 | | | |
| 10 | | | |

# Sentence ~ Subject + Be + Location

**Objective:** _____

| Target | | | |
|---|---|---|---|
| 1  He is in the car. | | | |
| 2  I am in the kitchen. | | | |
| 3  It is on the sink. | | | |
| 4  She is over there. | | | |
| 5  They are on the train. | | | |
| 6 | | | |
| 7 | | | |
| 8 | | | |
| 9 | | | |
| 10 | | | |

# Sentence ~ Subject + Be + Noun

**Objective:** _____

| Target | | | |
|---|---|---|---|
| 1  A banana is fruit. | | | |
| 2  A chair is furniture. | | | |
| 3  A giraffe is an animal. | | | |
| 4  Cake is a desert. | | | |
| 5 | | | |
| 6 | | | |

# Sentence ~ Subject + Be + Verb

**Objective:** _____

| | Target | | | |
|---|---|---|---|---|
| 1 | He has to work. | | | |
| 2 | He is drinking. | | | |
| 3 | I am playing. | | | |
| 4 | The birds are singing. | | | |
| 5 | The balls are bouncing. | | | |
| 6 | She is swinging. | | | |
| 7 | The dog is eating. | | | |
| 8 | The kids are painting. | | | |
| 9 | | | | |
| 10 | | | | |
| 11 | | | | |
| 12 | | | | |
| 13 | | | | |
| 14 | | | | |
| 15 | | | | |

# Sentence ~ Subject + Preposition + Noun

**Objective:** _____

| | Target | | | |
|---|---|---|---|---|
| 1 | He is at the beach. | | | |
| 2 | It is around the corner. | | | |
| 3 | The pencil is next to the book. | | | |
| 4 | She is in the kitchen. | | | |
| 5 | | | | |
| 6 | | | | |
| 7 | | | | |
| 8 | | | | |
| 9 | | | | |
| 10 | | | | |
| 11 | | | | |
| 12 | | | | |
| 13 | | | | |
| 14 | | | | |
| 15 | | | | |

# Sentence ~ Subject + Verb

**Objective:** _____

| Target | | | |
|---|---|---|---|
| 1  I clap. | | | |
| 2  She runs. | | | |
| 3  They sing. | | | |
| 4  The boy colors. | | | |
| 5  The girl reads. | | | |
| 6 | | | |
| 7 | | | |
| 8 | | | |
| 9 | | | |
| 10 | | | |

# Sentence ~ Subject + Verb + Location

**Objective:** _____

| Target | | | |
|---|---|---|---|
| 1  The man is in the boat. | | | |
| 2  The kids are riding in the bus. | | | |
| 3  The dog is sitting under the table. | | | |
| 4  The girl is climbing up the ladder. | | | |
| 5  They are swimming in the pool. | | | |
| 6 | | | |
| 7 | | | |
| 8 | | | |
| 9 | | | |

# Sentence ~ Subject + Verb + Noun

**Objective:** _____

| Target | | | |
|---|---|---|---|
| 1  He went down the slide | | | |
| 2  She rides a horse. | | | |
| 3  The boy colors a picture. | | | |
| 4  The dog jumps the fence. | | | |
| 5  The football player catches the ball. | | | |
| 6  The girl blows candles. | | | |

# Sentence ~ Subject + Verb + Noun

**Objective:** _____

| | Target | | | |
|---|---|---|---|---|
| 7 | The girl holds an umbrella. | | | |
| 8 | The girl reads a book. | | | |
| 9 | The girl throws the ball. | | | |
| 10 | The kids play a game. | | | |
| 11 | The man drinks water. | | | |
| 12 | The man walks the dog. | | | |
| 13 | | | | |
| 14 | | | | |
| 15 | | | | |
| 16 | | | | |
| 17 | | | | |
| 18 | | | | |
| 19 | | | | |
| 20 | | | | |

# Sentence ~ Subject + Verb + Noun + Location

**Objective:** _____

| | Target | | | |
|---|---|---|---|---|
| 1 | Mommy feeds the baby in the high chair. | | | |
| 2 | The boy went down the slide at the park. | | | |
| 3 | The girl sleeps in her bed. | | | |
| 4 | The girl floats on a raft in the pool. | | | |
| 5 | The girl raises her hand at school. | | | |
| 6 | The girl rides her bike outside. | | | |
| 7 | The kids play cars on the floor. | | | |
| 8 | The kids see Woody at Disneyland. | | | |
| 9 | The man puts the pizza in the oven. | | | |
| 10 | The woman buys groceries at the store. | | | |
| 11 | | | | |
| 12 | | | | |
| 13 | | | | |
| 14 | | | | |
| 15 | | | | |
| 16 | | | | |
| 17 | | | | |
| 18 | | | | |
| 19 | | | | |
| 20 | | | | |

# Sentence ~ Subject + Verb + Pronoun + Noun

**Objective:** _____

| Target | | | |
|---|---|---|---|
| 1  He waited his turn. | | | |
| 2  He is cleaning his room. | | | |
| 3  I put on my shirt. | | | |
| 4  I took my turn. | | | |
| 5  She fell off her bike. | | | |
| 6  She's wearing her hat. | | | |
| 7 | | | |
| 8 | | | |
| 9 | | | |
| 10 | | | |

# Sentence ~ Subject + Verb + Time

**Objective:** _____

| Target | | | |
|---|---|---|---|
| 1  He is going to school on Monday. | | | |
| 2  He is going to sing tomorrow. | | | |
| 3  I am going to read tonight. | | | |
| 4  She is going to camp in August. | | | |
| 5 | | | |
| 6 | | | |
| 7 | | | |
| 8 | | | |
| 9 | | | |
| 10 | | | |

**Objective:** _____

| Target | | | |
|---|---|---|---|
| 1 | | | |
| 2 | | | |
| 3 | | | |
| 4 | | | |
| 5 | | | |
| 6 | | | |
| 7 | | | |
| 8 | | | |

# Chapter 11 - Word Challenge
## Contraction

**Objective:** _____

| | Target | | | |
|---|---|---|---|---|
| 1 | can't – can not | | | |
| 2 | could've – could have | | | |
| 3 | doesn't – does not | | | |
| 4 | don't – do not | | | |
| 5 | he'd – he would | | | |
| 6 | he'll – he will | | | |
| 7 | here's – here is | | | |
| 8 | he's – he is | | | |
| 9 | I'd – I would | | | |
| 10 | I'm – I am | | | |
| 11 | isn't – is not | | | |
| 12 | it's – it is | | | |
| 13 | I've – I have | | | |
| 14 | let's – let us | | | |
| 15 | she'd – she would | | | |
| 16 | she'll – she will | | | |
| 17 | she's – she is | | | |
| 18 | should've – should have | | | |
| 19 | that's – that is | | | |
| 20 | there's – there is | | | |
| 21 | they're – they are | | | |
| 22 | they'd – they would | | | |
| 23 | they'll – they will | | | |
| 24 | we're – we are | | | |
| 25 | we've – we have | | | |
| 26 | what's – what is | | | |
| 27 | who's – who is | | | |
| 28 | won't – will not | | | |
| 29 | wouldn't – would not | | | |
| 30 | would've – would have | | | |
| 31 | you'd – you would | | | |
| 32 | you're – you are | | | |
| 33 | you've – you have | | | |
| 34 | | | | |
| 35 | | | | |
| 36 | | | | |
| 37 | | | | |
| 38 | | | | |
| 39 | | | | |

# Homograph

**Objective:** _____

| Target | | | |
|---|---|---|---|
| 1  ball - dance, toy | | | |
| 2  band - musicians, thin strip | | | |
| 3  bank - money, along river | | | |
| 4  bark - tree covering, dog | | | |
| 5  bat - mammal, club | | | |
| 6  bear - put weight on, animal | | | |
| 7  bit - small piece, drill | | | |
| 8  bow - weapon, ribbon, bend, ship | | | |
| 9  bowl - dish, sport | | | |
| 10  box - hit, container | | | |
| 11  brush - tool, action, bushes | | | |
| 12  buck - male deer, money | | | |
| 13  can - able to, metal object | | | |
| 14  chop - cut, piece of meat | | | |
| 15  close - shut, near | | | |
| 16  counter - person, table top | | | |
| 17  crow - loud cry, bird | | | |
| 18  date - time, fruit | | | |
| 19  desert - barren area, go away | | | |
| 20  duck - bird, go under | | | |
| 21  fan - blow air, person | | | |
| 22  felt - feel, cloth | | | |
| 23  flag - wave down, banner | | | |
| 24  fly - insect, move through air | | | |
| 25  gum - in mouth, chewing food | | | |
| 26  hide - animal, conceal | | | |
| 27  jam - push, sweet spread | | | |
| 28  jet - stream of water, airplane | | | |
| 29  lap - drink, body part, one trip around | | | |
| 30  last - at the end, continue | | | |
| 31  lean - stand, no fat | | | |
| 32  left - direction, did go | | | |
| 33  light - not dark, not heavy | | | |
| 34  like - similar, admire | | | |
| 35  nag - bug one, old horse | | | |
| 36  pool - game, tank of water | | | |
| 37  present - here, gift | | | |
| 38  punch - hit, drink | | | |
| 39  pupil - eye, student | | | |
| 40  racket - noise, tennis | | | |

# Homograph

**Objective:** _____

| | Target | | | |
|---|---|---|---|---|
| 41 | rest - sleep, what is left | | | |
| 42 | ring - circle, bell sound | | | |
| 43 | root - cheet, tree part | | | |
| 44 | row - line, use oars | | | |
| 45 | saw - did see, tool | | | |
| 46 | second - part of minute, after first | | | |
| 47 | shed - building, get rid of | | | |
| 48 | slip - piece of paper, fall | | | |
| 49 | slug - bug, hit | | | |
| 50 | sock - foot, hit hard | | | |
| 51 | soil - make dirty, dirt | | | |
| 52 | story - floor in building, book | | | |
| 53 | strip - piece of, remove | | | |
| 54 | tire - get sleepy, wheel | | | |
| 55 | top - up high, toy | | | |
| 56 | well - good, hole of water | | | |
| 57 | | | | |
| 58 | | | | |
| 59 | | | | |
| 60 | | | | |
| 61 | | | | |
| 62 | | | | |
| 63 | | | | |
| 64 | | | | |
| 65 | | | | |
| 66 | | | | |
| 67 | | | | |
| 68 | | | | |
| 69 | | | | |
| 70 | | | | |
| 71 | | | | |
| 72 | | | | |
| 73 | | | | |
| 74 | | | | |
| 75 | | | | |
| 76 | | | | |
| 77 | | | | |
| 78 | | | | |
| 79 | | | | |
| 80 | | | | |

# Homophone

**Objective:** _____

| Target | | | |
|---|---|---|---|
| 1  acts – ax | | | |
| 2  ad – add | | | |
| 3  aisle – I'll | | | |
| 4  allowed – aloud | | | |
| 5  ate – eight | | | |
| 6  bare – bear | | | |
| 7  be – bee | | | |
| 8  bean – been | | | |
| 9  beat – beet | | | |
| 10  blew – blue | | | |
| 11  buy – by – bye | | | |
| 12  ceiling – sealing | | | |
| 13  cent – sent | | | |
| 14  cheep – cheap | | | |
| 15  chews – choose | | | |
| 16  close – clothes | | | |
| 17  daze – days | | | |
| 18  deer – dear | | | |
| 19  dew – do | | | |
| 20  fairy – ferry | | | |
| 21  feet – feat | | | |
| 22  fir – fur | | | |
| 23  flea – flee | | | |
| 24  flew – flu | | | |
| 25  four – for | | | |
| 26  great – grate | | | |
| 27  gym – Jim | | | |
| 28  hair – hare | | | |
| 29  halve – have | | | |
| 30  hay – hey | | | |
| 31  hear – here | | | |
| 32  heard – herd | | | |
| 33  hi – high | | | |
| 34  hoarse – horse | | | |
| 35  hole – whole | | | |
| 36  I – eye | | | |
| 37  in – inn | | | |
| 38  kneed – need | | | |
| 39  knight – night | | | |
| 40  knot – not | | | |

# Homophone

**Objective:** _____

| Target | | | |
|---|---|---|---|
| 41 know – no | | | |
| 42 knows – nose | | | |
| 43 made – maid | | | |
| 44 mail – male | | | |
| 45 main – mane | | | |
| 46 manner – manor | | | |
| 47 marry – merry | | | |
| 48 meat – meet | | | |
| 49 missed – mist | | | |
| 50 muscle – mussel | | | |
| 51 oar – or | | | |
| 52 oh – owe | | | |
| 53 one – won | | | |
| 54 our – hour | | | |
| 55 pair – pare | | | |
| 56 pane – pain | | | |
| 57 passed – past | | | |
| 58 pea – pee | | | |
| 59 peek – peak | | | |
| 60 peer –pier | | | |
| 61 piece – peace | | | |
| 62 poor – pour | | | |
| 63 pray – prey | | | |
| 64 prince – prints | | | |
| 65 rain – reign | | | |
| 66 rap – wrap | | | |
| 67 read – reed | | | |
| 68 right – write | | | |
| 69 road – rode | | | |
| 70 role – roll | | | |
| 71 rose – rows | | | |
| 72 sail – sale | | | |
| 73 sea – see | | | |
| 74 seem – seam | | | |
| 75 seen – scene | | | |
| 76 sew – so | | | |
| 77 shoe – shoo | | | |
| 78 soar – sore | | | |
| 79 some – sum | | | |
| 80 stair – stare | | | |

# Homophone

**Objective:** _____

| | Target | | | |
|---|---|---|---|---|
| 81 | stake – steak | | | |
| 82 | sundae – Sunday | | | |
| 83 | tail – tale | | | |
| 84 | their – there | | | |
| 85 | through – threw | | | |
| 86 | tied – tide | | | |
| 87 | to – too – two | | | |
| 88 | toe – tow | | | |
| 89 | wail – whale | | | |
| 90 | waist – waste | | | |
| 91 | wait – weight | | | |
| 92 | warn – worn | | | |
| 93 | way – weigh | | | |
| 94 | weather – whether | | | |
| 95 | weed – we'd | | | |
| 96 | week – weak | | | |
| 97 | we're – were | | | |
| 98 | where – ware – wear | | | |
| 99 | which – witch | | | |
| 100 | would – wood | | | |
| 101 | wring – ring | | | |
| 102 | | | | |
| 103 | | | | |
| 104 | | | | |
| 105 | | | | |
| 106 | | | | |
| 107 | | | | |
| 108 | | | | |
| 109 | | | | |
| 110 | | | | |
| 111 | | | | |
| 112 | | | | |
| 113 | | | | |
| 114 | | | | |
| 115 | | | | |
| 116 | | | | |
| 117 | | | | |
| 118 | | | | |
| 119 | | | | |
| 120 | | | | |

# Idiom

**Objective:** _____

| | Target | | | |
|---|---|---|---|---|
| 1 | All the time. | | | |
| 2 | As soon as possible | | | |
| 3 | Bring up. | | | |
| 4 | By the way | | | |
| 5 | Call it a day. | | | |
| 6 | Cool it. | | | |
| 7 | Cut it out. | | | |
| 8 | Don't bug me. | | | |
| 9 | Easy does it. | | | |
| 10 | Go for it. | | | |
| 11 | Hurry up. | | | |
| 12 | I changed my mind. | | | |
| 13 | I really mean it. | | | |
| 14 | In a little bit | | | |
| 15 | In the first place | | | |
| 16 | Inside out | | | |
| 17 | Its about time. | | | |
| 18 | It's out of hand. | | | |
| 19 | It's too high. | | | |
| 20 | Keep an eye on it. | | | |
| 21 | Never mind. | | | |
| 22 | On the other hand | | | |
| 23 | Over your head. | | | |
| 24 | Sick and tired | | | |
| 25 | Step on it. | | | |
| 26 | Take it easy. | | | |
| 27 | Take your time. | | | |
| 28 | That's weird. | | | |
| 29 | There it goes | | | |
| 30 | You're chicken. | | | |
| 31 | | | | |
| 32 | | | | |
| 33 | | | | |
| 34 | | | | |
| 35 | | | | |
| 36 | | | | |
| 37 | | | | |
| 38 | | | | |
| 39 | | | | |
| 40 | | | | |

# Chapter 12 - Talk About Topic

The Talk About Topic provides a list of related information on a topic. These are used to:

1. Take turns making a comment about a topic.
2. Ask questions and provide answers about a topic.
3. Make up short stories about a topic.
4. Have a conversation about a topic.

You can create additional topics by asking these questions about the topic.

What color is it?
What do you do there?
What do you use it for?
What does he drink?
What does he play with?
What does he say?
What does it do?
What does it eat?
What does she like?
What does she wear?
What is a XYZ?
What movie is he in?
Where do you do it?
Where do you see it?
Where does it go?
Where does it live?
Where does it sleep?
What does it have?
What does it look like?
Is it a girl or a boy?
When do you do it?
How many legs does he have?
Who is his friend?

# Activities

| Go to Bed | Wake Up |
|---|---|
| take a bath | open eyes |
| put on pajamas | stretch arms and legs |
| brush teeth | say "good morning" |
| go to the bathroom | get out of bed |
| read a book | go to the bathroom |
| put head on pillow | get dressed |
| get under the covers | eat breakfast |
| close your eyes & go to sleep | |

| Go to School | Eat Dinner |
|---|---|
| wait for the bus | set the table |
| get on the bus | get the food |
| go in to school | eat with a fork |
| hang up coat | cut with knife |
| put away backpack | use napkin |
| say "hi" to teacher | eat food & have a drink |
| say "hi" to friends | clean up dishes |
| | use manners |

| Play Tag | Beach |
|---|---|
| play with kids | wear swim suit |
| chase the kid | play in the sand |
| tag his shoulder | build a sand castle |
| run away fast | splash in the water |
| say "you're it" | put on sunscreen |
| play in the grass | sit on the blanket |
| | dry off with a towel |
| | use a pail and shovel |
| | wear sunglasses |

| Camping | Picnic |
|---|---|
| set up a tent | sit on a blanket |
| camp in the forest | go to a park |
| make a fire | drink lemonade |
| roast marshmallows | eat sandwich |
| zip up sleeping bag | play Frisbee |
| see the stars at night | rest in the sun |
| walk in the woods | |

| Birthday | Movies |
|---|---|
| sing "Happy Birthday" | drive to the theatre |
| blow out candles | buy tickets |
| get presents | get popcorn |
| eat birthday cake | buy candy |
| eat ice cream | find seats |
| play games | be quiet |
| say "Thank you" for presents | watch the movie |

# Animals

| Horse | Dog |
|---|---|
| is a farm animal | barks |
| people ride | says woof woof |
| says neigh | 4 legs |
| lives on a farm | tail |
| wears a saddle | runs |
| has a mane | eats meat |
| has a tail | likes to get pet |
| has 4 legs | is a pet |
| gets brush | lives in a house |
| eats grass | is an animal |
| eats hay | has paws |
| drinks water | walk a dog |
| wears horse shoes | wears a leash |
| pulls a wagon | can bite people |

| Cow | Cat |
|---|---|
| makes milk | purrs |
| says moo | says meow |
| eats grass | has whiskers |
| lives on a farm | has 4 paws |
| is a farm animal | long tail |
| is big | drinks milk |
| has 4 legs | eats cat food |
| has an udder | jumps up |
| has a tail | is a pet |
| drinks water | lives in a house |

| Zebra | Elephant |
|---|---|
| has black stripes | has big ears |
| has a white body | is grey |
| looks like a horse | has 4 legs |
| has a tail | has a trunk |
| lives in a zoo | has a tail |
| eats grass | eats hay |
| has 4 legs | lives at the zoo |

| Whale | Fish |
|---|---|
| is an ocean animal | eats plants |
| is a big mammal | lives in the water |
| eats little fish | swims around |
| swims in the ocean | can be a pet |
| splash the water | has gills |
| has a tail | some people eat fish |

# Animals

| Bird | Bear |
|---|---|
| lives in the forest | lives in the forest |
| sleeps in a nest | eats honey |
| makes a nest from sticks | eats plants or meat |
| eats worms | sleeps in the winter |
| flys in the sky | is big animal |
| has wings | is black or brown |
| has a tail | has 4 legs |
| is a small animal | can walk on 2 legs |
| there are many kinds of birds | is fat |
| says tweet tweet | has fur |
| **Bee** | **Spider** |
| makes honey | is an insect |
| say buzz | is black |
| is an insect | have many legs |
| flys in the sky | crawl in the house |
| can sting people | live outside |
| is small | scare people |
| help flowers grow | makes a web |
| live outside | eats insects |
| **Frog** | **Giraffe** |
| has two eyes | has a long neck |
| likes the water | has pointy eyes |
| can be green or brown | eats grass |
| likes to jump | lives in Africa |
| says ribbit | lives at the zoo |
| lives near a pond | is very tall |
| has 4 legs | has 4 long legs |
| **Turtle** | **Squirrel** |
| has a hard shell | has a brushy tail |
| likes the water | has two eyes |
| walks very slow | eats acorns |
| is green or brown | lives in the forest |
| has a little tail | runs up a tree |
| has 4 legs | is gray |
|  | has fur |

# Art

| Paint | Scissors |
|---|---|
| comes in colors<br>makes a picture<br>put on a brush<br>is wet<br>need to cover when done<br>is messy<br>can stain clothing | are sharp<br>open and close<br>have a handle<br>have blades<br>used for cutting<br>handle carefully<br>cuts paper |
| **Glue** | **Paper** |
| is sticky<br>is white<br>squeeze it out<br>put on paper<br>sticks things together | is flat<br>comes in many colors<br>can write on<br>can draw on<br>can cut shapes from |
| **Crayons** | **Tape** |
| used for drawing<br>use on paper<br>come in many colors<br>made of wax<br>are sharpened<br>hold in your hands<br>store in a box | is clear<br>is sticky<br>used to put stuff together<br>fixes a tear<br>have to rip it<br>put on paper<br>used for wrapping a present |
| **Pencil** | **Eraser** |
| is a writing tool<br>must be sharpened<br>has black lead<br>made of wood<br>writes on paper<br>has an eraser | on the end of a pencil<br>fixes mistake<br>rub on paper<br>makes marks disappear<br>is flaky |

# Disney Characters

| Cinderella | Woody |
|---|---|
| princess<br>has a blue dress<br>dances with the prince<br>lives in a castle<br>has white gloves<br>has long blond hair<br>is a girl | is a cowboy<br>has a friend named Buzz<br>is in the movie Toy Story<br>has a hat<br>wears boots<br>rides a horse<br>says "Howdy, Partner" |
| **Tarzan** | **Dumbo** |
| lives in a jungle<br>swings from trees<br>eats meat<br>has brown hair<br>is a man | is an elephant<br>has big ears<br>has a trunk<br>flies in the sky<br>he is in the circus |
| **Lion King** | **Snow White** |
| is a movie<br>lions live in Africa<br>mean lion is named Scar<br>lions eat meat<br>lions names were Simba and Nala<br>Simba likes to run and pounce | is a princess<br>gets kissed by the prince<br>eats a poisoned apple<br>lives with 7 dwarfs<br>sings with the birds<br>is a girl<br>helps the dwarfs with manners |
| **Pooh** | **Hunchback** |
| pooh is a bear<br>he eats honey<br>he is fat<br>his friend is Piglet<br>lives in the 100 acre woods<br>wears a red shirt | he rings bells in Notre Dame<br>lives in a castle<br>his friend is Esmeralda<br>he is in Hunchback of Notre Dame<br>the movie has gargoyles<br>his name is Quasimodo |
| **Ariel** | **Pocahontas** |
| has red hair<br>lives in the sea<br>is a mermaid<br>is a girl<br>her friend is Sebastian | is an Indian<br>lives in the forest<br>her friend is John Smith<br>has black hair<br>her friend is Meeko |
| **Mickey Mouse** | **Aladdin** |
| is a mouse<br>has big ears<br>is friends with Minnie Mouse<br>wears white gloves<br>has a tail<br>likes to laugh | is a boy<br>rides a magic carpet<br>is friends with a princess Jasmine<br>has a monkey named Abu<br>rubs a magic lamp<br>has black hair |

# Food

| Apple | Hot Dog |
|---|---|
| red or green<br>is a fruit<br>has skin<br>crunches<br>eat it<br>is a snack | is meat<br>is brown<br>eat for lunch<br>put on ketchup<br>is long<br>eat in a bun |
| **Banana** | **Cake** |
| is yellow<br>is a fruit<br>is soft<br>has a peel<br>eat it<br>peel it<br>it is a healthy snack | is a desert<br>is sweet<br>has icing<br>eat at a birthday party<br>can have candles<br>get a piece<br>bake in the oven |
| **Cookies** | **Cereal** |
| are round<br>are sweet<br>are crunchy<br>bake in the oven<br>are a desert<br>have chocolate chips<br>are small | is a food<br>rat it with a spoon<br>put it in a bowl<br>pour on milk<br>it is crunchy<br>eat it for breakfast<br>comes in a box |
| **Carrots** | **Bacon** |
| are a vegetable<br>are orange<br>are crunchy<br>grow under ground<br>eat in a salad<br>are a good snack | is brown<br>is greasy<br>is meat<br>fry in a pan<br>have for breakfast<br>is crunchy |
| **Hamburger** | **Candy** |
| is round<br>is meat<br>put on a bun<br>put ketchup on it<br>get at a restaurant<br>is greasy<br>is brown | is sweet<br>is for desert<br>comes in many colors<br>can be hard<br>is delicious<br>can be chewy<br>eat just a little |

# Food

| Egg | Chips |
|---|---|
| is a food<br>eat for breakfast<br>fry in a pan<br>is round<br>is white and yellow<br>can have it scrambled | are a snack<br>Is food<br>are salty<br>are crunchy<br>are white<br>come in a bag |
| **Ice Cream** | **Juice** |
| is a desert<br>is cold<br>can be chocolate<br>comes in a cone<br>eat it<br>lick it<br>is made from milk<br>taste sweet | is a drink<br>made from fruit<br>pour it in a cup<br>can be orange<br>can be apple<br>have with breakfast<br>drink it<br>have it cold |
| **Milk** | **Orange** |
| is a drink<br>comes from cows<br>is white<br>is cold<br>kept in the refrigerator<br>pour on cereal<br>drink from a glass | is a fruit<br>grows on a tree<br>has a peel<br>is juicy<br>it is round<br>you peel it<br>you eat it |
| **French Fries** | **Peas** |
| are a food<br>made from potatoes<br>are white<br>are greasy<br>taste salty<br>eat with your fingers<br>get at McDonalds | are small<br>are green<br>are a vegetable<br>eat them<br>have for dinner<br>are round<br>taste sweet |
| **Bread** | **Pretzels** |
| make sandwiches<br>is sliced<br>has a crust<br>is white<br>can be toasted<br>is chewy<br>have for lunch | are salty<br>have a twisted shape<br>are brown<br>eat as a snack<br>are crunchy<br>come in a bag |

# Holiday

| Easter | Valentine's Day |
|---|---|
| hunt for eggs | make red hearts |
| boil eggs | give presents |
| dye and paint eggs | say "I love you" |
| see the easter bunny | give cards |
| get a chocolate bunny | say "Be my valentine" |
| get an Easter basket | eat chocolate |
| see Easter lily | have a party |
| eat jelly beans | |

| Christmas | Halloween |
|---|---|
| is on December 25th | is on October 31st |
| Ssanta Claus comes | I wear a costume |
| we give presents | a witch flies on a broom |
| we get presents | I see ghosts |
| we decorate the Christmas tree | we carve pumpkins |
| we eat a big dinner | I say "trick or treat" |
| we go to church | I knock on doors |
| Christmas is in the winter | I get candy |

| Thanksgiving | Fourth of July |
|---|---|
| you eat turkey | go to a parade |
| have a big dinner | see fire works |
| visit with relatives | carry the American flag |
| give thanks for your things | wear red, white and blue |
| have pumpkin pie | go to a carnival |
| eat cranberry sauce | have a picnic |
| | eat hot dogs |
| | celebrate America |

# Household

| Bed | Chair |
|---|---|
| is furniture<br>you sleep in it<br>has sheets<br>has a pillow<br>has blankets<br>found in the bedroom | is furniture<br>has legs<br>has a seat<br>has arms<br>you sit on it<br>goes with a table |
| **Clock** | **Computer** |
| has batteries<br>has hands<br>tells time<br>on the wall<br>has numbers | turn it on<br>play games on it<br>has a mouse<br>has a keyboard<br>it is a machine |
| **Refrigerator** | **Knife** |
| is an appliance<br>keeps food cold<br>in the kitchen<br>is cold<br>has milk and meat<br>has a door<br>plugs in to the wall | is a piece of silverware<br>use it to cut food<br>it is sharp<br>we are careful with it<br>keep it in the drawer<br>has a handle<br>goes with a fork |
| **Shampoo** | **Telephone** |
| is a cleaning product<br>found in the bathroom<br>used to clean hair<br>mixed with water<br>makes bubbles<br>comes in a bottle<br>squeeze out | has numbers<br>has a cord<br>has buttons<br>goes ring ring<br>talk on<br>say "hello"<br>in the kitchen |
| **Oven** | **Cup** |
| is hot<br>is an appliance<br>in the kitchen<br>cooks food<br>is white<br>has a door<br>has buttons<br>is electrical | is for liquids<br>gets filled up<br>in the kitchen<br>gets empty<br>you drink from<br>put in juice<br>put in water<br>washed in the sink |

# Occupations

| Police Officer | Farmer |
|---|---|
| wear a suit | works on a farm |
| wear a hat | grows food |
| carry a gun | weeds the garden |
| help people | drives a tractor |
| drive a police car | feeds the chicken |
| fight crime | weeds the garden |
|  | milks the cows |
| **Fire Fighter** | **Waiter** |
| wears a fire proof suit | gives you a menu |
| drives a fire truck | takes your order |
| uses a fire hose | brings you to your seat |
| sprays water | gives you food |
| puts out fires | pours your water |
| climbs a ladder | works in a restaurant |
| **Doctor** | **Dentist** |
| helps sick people | wears a mask |
| works in the hospital | cleans your teeth |
| gives you medicine | gives you a new tooth brush |
| checks your temperature | works in an office |
| wears a white coat | has a big chair |
| looks in your mouth | uses dental floss |
| looks in your ears | talks to mom and dad |
| weighs you | wears gloves |
| talks to mom and dad | has bright lights |
| **Pilot** | **Teacher** |
| flys an airplane | works at the school |
| wears a uniform | teaches children |
| has a hat | gives you lessons |
| sits in the cockpit | reads you books |
| uses the controls | likes children |
| talks to people on the airplane | teaches how to read |
| lands the airplane |  |
| **Lifeguard** | **Cook** |
| wears a bathing suit | works in the kitchen |
| saves swimmers | makes people food |
| works at a pool | mixes food |
| swims in the water | uses the stove |
| says "no running" | puts pans in the oven |
| watches the people | wears an apron |
| keeps people safe | chops vegetables |

# Outside

| House | Flower |
|---|---|
| has doors<br>has windows<br>has a roof<br>is where people live<br>has rooms<br>has a garage<br>is in a neighborhood<br>has a yard | grows outside<br>has a stem<br>has petals<br>smells nice<br>looks pretty<br>is a plant<br>needs water<br>grows in the dirt<br>put in a vase |
| **Grass** | **Moon** |
| is green<br>is in the backyard<br>gets mowed<br>has weeds<br>is long and thin<br>need to water it | is in the sky<br>can see at night<br>is bright<br>is big<br>shines light<br>is different shapes<br>is in space |
| **Rain** | **Ocean** |
| falls from the sky<br>made from the clouds<br>gets you wet<br>falls on the ground<br>makes puddles<br>is a type of weather | is full of water<br>has fish<br>has whales<br>is salty<br>has a beach<br>has waves<br>can swim in |
| **Snow** | **Sun** |
| is white<br>is cold<br>is a type of weather<br>falls in the winter<br>used to make a snowman<br>people ski on it<br>people slide on it | is hot<br>is yellow<br>shines in the sky<br>is in space<br>makes the daytime<br>is bright |

# PBS Characters

| Madeline | Arthur |
|---|---|
| is a girl | wears glasses |
| has red hair | his sister is DW |
| has a yellow hat | his friend is Buster |
| has a little dog | his puppy is Pal |
| likes lemonaide | likes to eat chocolate birthday cake |
| wears a blue coat | plays computer games |
| **Barney** | **Clifford** |
| is a purple dinosaur | is a big red dog |
| likes to sing | his friend is Emily Elizabeth |
| his friend is BJ | has floppy ears |
| his friend is Baby Bop | has a long tail |
| he sings "I love you" | he eats bones |
| he is on TV | likes to play with kids |

# Places

| Playground | McDonalds |
|---|---|
| go down the slide | has golden arches |
| climb up the ladder | has a playland |
| run around | play with the kids |
| go up and down on see saw | jump in the ball pit |
| climb the monkey bars | buy a happy meal |
| play in the sand | eat a burger |
| play with kids | get French fries |
| **Library** | **Grocery Store** |
| look at books | push a shopping cart |
| check out videos | look at vegetables |
| borrow books | get potato chips |
| get CDs | buy meat |
| be quiet | pick out apples |
| listen to a story | put fruit in a bag |
| | buy the food |

# Places

| Zoo | Farm |
|---|---|
| has wild animals<br>animals live in cages<br>animals behind fences<br>go to the gift shop<br>don't feed the animals<br>monkeys make noises | see a barn<br>look at cows<br>feed the chickens<br>watch the horses run<br>sheep are behind the fence<br>rabbits are in a cage |
| **Space** | **Restaurant** |
| space has planets<br>earth is a planet<br>we live on earth<br>astronauts fly in space<br>astronauts wear white suits<br>astronauts fly space shuttle<br>space shuttle goes blast off | eat food<br>sit on seat<br>drink water<br>go to the bathroom<br>read the menu<br>get burger and fries<br>give order to waiter |
| **Mall** | **Store** |
| ride the elevator<br>go up the escalator<br>walk around<br>go to the Disney store<br>get a snack<br>go shopping<br>sit on the bench | look for toys or clothes<br>play with toys<br>put on clothes<br>buy the toys<br>pay with money or credit card<br>get a bag<br>say "Thank You" |
| **Gas Station** | **Post Office** |
| drive to the gas pump<br>pick up the gas pump<br>put in the gas<br>pay for the gas<br>get a snack inside<br>wash the car windows | park in the parking lot<br>go into the post office<br>wait in line<br>talk to the postal clerk<br>buy stamps<br>mail letters<br>send off package |
| **Airport** | **School** |
| where airplanes land<br>where airplanes take off<br>check you baggage<br>where you get on airplane<br>fly in the airplane<br>eat food at the airport<br>pick up people<br>ride the escalator | has classrooms<br>kids learn at school<br>has teachers<br>go to lunch<br>have recess<br>go to the library<br>read books<br>write stories |

# Seasons

| Summer | Autumn |
|---|---|
| wear shorts | it gets cooler |
| go to the park | the leaves turn color |
| wear sunscreen | the leaves fall |
| wear sunglasses | it gets windy |
| go swimming | we have Halloween |
| see leaves on the trees | we rake leaves |
| play in the sprinkler | wear a coat |
| turn on air conditioning | is called Fall |
| use the fan | go back to school |
| **Winter** | **Spring** |
| it is cold | it rains |
| it snows | the flowers bloom |
| wear a coat and hat | the grass grows |
| wear boots and mittens | the birds tweet |
| make a snowman | use an umbrella |
| play in the snow | wear a rain coat |
| see snowflakes | splash in the puddles |

# Sports

| Baseball | Soccer |
|---|---|
| swing a bat | throw a soccer ball |
| throw a ball | kick a soccer ball |
| run the bases | play on a team |
| catch the ball | make a goal |
| play on a team | run down the field |
| wear a baseball cap | |

| Basketball | Tennis |
|---|---|
| throw a basketball | swing the tennis racket |
| make a basket | run after the ball |
| shoot for the hoop | hit the ball |
| run down the court | play on the tennis court |
| play on a team | play with another person |
| wear shorts | wear tennis shoes |
| wear sneakers | |

| Football | Golf |
|---|---|
| played on a football field | played on a big course |
| has teams | use golf clubs |
| played by football players | hit a little white ball |
| uses a brown ball | shoot the ball into a hole |
| ball gets kicked | played on the grass |
| players fall down | |

| Swimming | Hockey |
|---|---|
| go to the pool | played with a stick |
| play with a torpedo | shoot a puck |
| wear a floaty | get a goal |
| throw a ball | wear a helmet |
| jump in the water | wear padding |
| wear goggles | wear gloves |
| take a shower | wear skates |
| dry off with a towel | play on ice |
| get dressed | |

| Ski | Volleyball |
|---|---|
| wear skis | hit a ball |
| wear boots | go over the net |
| go on the snow | play on a team |
| do in the winter | use a white volleyball |
| go to the ski resort | try to score |
| go down the hill fast | use your hands |
| ride up in a chair | don't let it hit the ground |

# Things

| Book | Flashlight |
|---|---|
| has pages | turns on |
| has words | turns off |
| has pictures | makes light |
| read it | use in the dark |
| it tells a story | has a switch |
| open it | uses batteries |
| close it | helps you see at night |
| turn the pages | use when camping |
| **Fingers** | **Elevator** |
| have 5 on each hand | goes up |
| one is a thumb | goes down |
| have nails | has buttons |
| have knuckles | stops on floors |
| use to touch things | has a door |
| wear rings | carries people |
| can bend | has a bell |
| can make a fist | is in a building |
| **Piano** | **Key** |
| is an instrument | opens locks |
| makes music | use in a door |
| is black | made of metal |
| has white and black keys | keep on a key chain |
| gets played | use to drive a car |
| has a bench | carry in your pocket |
| is in an orchestra | |
| is big | |
| **VCR** | **TV** |
| plays videos | has shows |
| plugs into the TV | plugs into the wall |
| plugs into the socket | has a screen |
| has buttons | has a remote control |
| is an electronic | has buttons |
| needs electricity | gets turned on |
| has a remote control | gets turned off |
| plays movies | |

# Vehicles

| Airplane | Car |
|---|---|
| pilot flys | has 4 wheels |
| carries people places | has a trunk |
| takes off from airport | has doors |
| flys in the sky | has windows |
| lands on the ground | has an engine |
| has a tail | carries people |
| has wings | drives on the street |
| is a big vehicle | parks in a parking lot |
| has loud engines | goes in the garage |
| **Bike** | **Motorcycle** |
| has 2 wheels | has 2 wheels |
| has handle bars | has an engine |
| you ride it | is noisy |
| it is fun | drives on the street |
| has a chain | carries 1 or 2 people |
| has pedals | need to wear a helmet |
| need to wear a helmet | goes fast |
| **Fire Truck** | **Ambulance** |
| is a vehicle | is a vehicle |
| has ladders | has a siren |
| has a siren | has a driver |
| has a driver | has wheels |
| has wheels | goes fast |
| goes fast | carries sick people |
| carries fire fighters | goes to the hospital |
| has hoses | has medicine |
| parks at a fire station | has emergency workers |
| **Train** | **Boat** |
| goes on a train track | floats in the water |
| has an engine | carries people |
| carries people | some have a sail |
| has a caboose | some have a motor |
| has an engineer | get wet |
| is long | go in the ocean |
| has many cars | used for fishing |
| carries things | |

# References

Leaf, R., McEachin, J. (1999). A Work in Progress. New York, NY. DRL Books, L.L.C.

Maurice, C., Green, G., Luce, S.C. (1996). Behavioral Intervention For Young Children with Autism. Austin, TX. ProEd, Inc.

Partington, J.W., Sundberg, M.L. (1998). The Assessment of Basic Language and Learning Skills. Danville, CA. Behavior Analysts, Inc.

Sundberg, M.L., Partington, J.W. (1998). Teaching Language to Children with Autism or Other Developmental Disabilitites. Danville, CA. Behavior Analysts, Inc.

# Index

# Index

# Index

# Index

| | | | | |
|---|---|---|---|---|
| 1 | | | | |
| 2 | | | | |
| 3 | | | | |
| 4 | | | | |
| 5 | | | | |
| 6 | | | | |
| 7 | | | | |
| 8 | | | | |
| 9 | | | | |
| 10 | | | | |
| 11 | | | | |
| 12 | | | | |
| 13 | | | | |
| 14 | | | | |
| 15 | | | | |
| 16 | | | | |
| 17 | | | | |
| 18 | | | | |
| 19 | | | | |
| 20 | | | | |
| 21 | | | | |
| 22 | | | | |
| 23 | | | | |
| 24 | | | | |
| 25 | | | | |
| 26 | | | | |
| 27 | | | | |
| 28 | | | | |
| 29 | | | | |
| 30 | | | | |
| 31 | | | | |
| 32 | | | | |
| 33 | | | | |
| 34 | | | | |
| 35 | | | | |
| 36 | | | | |
| 37 | | | | |
| 38 | | | | |
| 39 | | | | |
| 40 | | | | |

Language Targets to Teach a Child to Communicate

| | | | | |
|---|---|---|---|---|
| 1 | | | | |
| 2 | | | | |
| 3 | | | | |
| 4 | | | | |
| 5 | | | | |
| 6 | | | | |
| 7 | | | | |
| 8 | | | | |
| 9 | | | | |
| 10 | | | | |
| 11 | | | | |
| 12 | | | | |
| 13 | | | | |
| 14 | | | | |
| 15 | | | | |
| 16 | | | | |
| 17 | | | | |
| 18 | | | | |
| 19 | | | | |
| 20 | | | | |
| 21 | | | | |
| 22 | | | | |
| 23 | | | | |
| 24 | | | | |
| 25 | | | | |
| 26 | | | | |
| 27 | | | | |
| 28 | | | | |
| 29 | | | | |
| 30 | | | | |
| 31 | | | | |
| 32 | | | | |
| 33 | | | | |
| 34 | | | | |
| 35 | | | | |
| 36 | | | | |
| 37 | | | | |
| 38 | | | | |
| 39 | | | | |
| 40 | | | | |

| | | | | |
|---|---|---|---|---|
| 1 | | | | |
| 2 | | | | |
| 3 | | | | |
| 4 | | | | |
| 5 | | | | |
| 6 | | | | |
| 7 | | | | |
| 8 | | | | |
| 9 | | | | |
| 10 | | | | |
| 11 | | | | |
| 12 | | | | |
| 13 | | | | |
| 14 | | | | |
| 15 | | | | |
| 16 | | | | |
| 17 | | | | |
| 18 | | | | |
| 19 | | | | |
| 20 | | | | |
| 21 | | | | |
| 22 | | | | |
| 23 | | | | |
| 24 | | | | |
| 25 | | | | |
| 26 | | | | |
| 27 | | | | |
| 28 | | | | |
| 29 | | | | |
| 30 | | | | |
| 31 | | | | |
| 32 | | | | |
| 33 | | | | |
| 34 | | | | |
| 35 | | | | |
| 36 | | | | |
| 37 | | | | |
| 38 | | | | |
| 39 | | | | |
| 40 | | | | |

Language Targets to Teach a Child to Communicate

| | | | | |
|---|---|---|---|---|
| 1 | | | | |
| 2 | | | | |
| 3 | | | | |
| 4 | | | | |
| 5 | | | | |
| 6 | | | | |
| 7 | | | | |
| 8 | | | | |
| 9 | | | | |
| 10 | | | | |
| 11 | | | | |
| 12 | | | | |
| 13 | | | | |
| 14 | | | | |
| 15 | | | | |
| 16 | | | | |
| 17 | | | | |
| 18 | | | | |
| 19 | | | | |
| 20 | | | | |
| 21 | | | | |
| 22 | | | | |
| 23 | | | | |
| 24 | | | | |
| 25 | | | | |
| 26 | | | | |
| 27 | | | | |
| 28 | | | | |
| 29 | | | | |
| 30 | | | | |
| 31 | | | | |
| 32 | | | | |
| 33 | | | | |
| 34 | | | | |
| 35 | | | | |
| 36 | | | | |
| 37 | | | | |
| 38 | | | | |
| 39 | | | | |
| 40 | | | | |

Language Targets to Teach a Child to Communicate